Table of Contents

Calling to the Heart

Medjugorje in Faith and Tradition

by

Dr. ant

Contents

Preamble

The small village of Medjugorje in Bosnia and Herzegovina has garnered international attention since the reported apparitions of the Virgin Mary began in 1981. Over the decades, Medjugorje has become a significant pilgrimage site for Catholics, drawing millions who seek spiritual enlightenment and connection with the divine. However, the status of these alleged apparitions has been a subject of controversy and scrutiny within the Catholic Church. Recently, the Dicastery for the Doctrine of the Faith (DDF) issued a statement regarding Medjugorje, signaling a pivotal moment in the Church's approach to the phenomenon. This essay explores the history of the Medjugorje apparitions, the Church's responses over the years, and the critical clarifications made by the Dicastery.

Historical Background

The Medjugorje apparitions began on June 24, 1981, when six children—Mirjana, Ivanka, Vicka, Jakov, and the twins, Maria and Milka—reported seeing a vision of a woman who identified herself as the Blessed Virgin Mary. Over the following months, these children claimed to have had numerous encounters with Mary, who imparted messages of peace, prayer, conversion, and penance. As news of these events spread, Medjugorje quickly became a focal point for the faithful, as well as a site of skepticism and inquiry from Church authorities.

The local bishop, Pavao Žanić, expressed reservations about the authenticity of the apparitions, leading to a complex relationship between the Church and the Medjugorje phenomenon. In 1991, the Yugoslav Bishops' Conference established a commission to investigate the claims. This commission was followed by a more extensive investigation led by the Vatican in 2010, called the "International Commission on Medjugorje." In 2014, Pope Francis authorized a new approach to the site, allowing officially sanctioned pilgrimages to Medjugorje while withholding definitive approval of the apparitions themselves.

Recent Developments and the Dicastery's Approval

In May 2020, the Vatican announced the establishment of a new pastoral framework for the Medjugorje site. A significant development occurred in December 2022 when the Dicastery for the Doctrine of the Faith issued a statement recognizing the spiritual fruits that have emerged from Medjugorje. The statement emphasized that the experiences of the pilgrims and the community were valid and beneficial for the Church, indicating a level of pastoral acceptance.

However, the Dicastery clarified that while the spiritual impact of Medjugorje is acknowledged, the apparitions themselves have not been fully authenticated by the Church. This distinction is crucial, as it implies that the Church does not endorse the supernatural nature of the claims made by the seers. Instead, the focus is on the positive outcomes of pilgrimage and devotion that have emerged from the site, which include increased prayer, reconciliation, and a deeper commitment to faith.

Clarifications on the Seers and Apparitions

The Dicastery's statement clarified that while Mary is believed to be appearing in Medjugorje, the authenticity of the seers' claims and the specific details of the apparitions remain under scrutiny. The ongoing investigation into the nature of the apparitions is critical, as the Church requires rigorous examination before affirming any supernatural claims.

The seers themselves have undergone various experiences, with some reporting ongoing visions and messages from Mary. However, the Church maintains that these experiences must be approached with caution. The faithful are encouraged to discern these messages in light of Church teaching and to focus on their spiritual growth, rather than solely on the phenomenon of the apparitions.

Conclusion

The Dicastery's recent approval of Medjugorje as a site of pilgrimage marks an important chapter in the ongoing story of the apparitions. While acknowledging the spiritual fruits resulting from the Medjugorje experience, the Church has not definitively authenticated the claims of the seers or the nature of the apparitions. This careful approach underscores the Church's commitment to ensuring that any acceptance of supernatural claims is grounded in thorough investigation and discernment. As millions continue to visit Medjugorje, the emphasis remains on fostering a genuine spiritual journey, rooted in faith, prayer, and community, rather than a singular focus on the miraculous. Thus, the legacy of Medjugorje continues to unfold, inviting the faithful to explore their relationship with the divine in light of both tradition and contemporary experience.

Introduction

The phenomenon of Medjugorje invites us into a sacred narrative, beckoning those who seek to understand its profound mystery. It is a tale that transcends the ordinary, delving into the realms where the earthly meets the celestial. The small village of Medjugorje, nestled in the heart of Bosnia and Herzegovina, has become a beacon for the faithful and the curious alike, drawing pilgrims from every corner of the globe. Here, the veil between heaven and earth is said to thin, offering glimpses of the divine through apparitions of the Virgin Mary. This introduction sets the stage for a journey not only geographical but deeply spiritual and transformative.

From the outset, Medjugorje is not just another geographical location; it is a place deeply entrenched in the history of Catholic spirituality. The visions reported by the seers have sparked a phenomenon that includes both faith and skepticism, celebration and controversy. Despite the varied reactions, these apparitions, reported since 1981, compel us to ask: What is their significance? How do they align with the sacred traditions and scriptures that have guided the Church for centuries? This book endeavors to answer these questions, offering a thoughtful examination of the messages delivered in Medjugorje and their implications for today.

To Roman Catholics, biblical scholars, and spiritualists, the study of apparitional sites similar to Medjugorje comes with a multitude of meanings. In understanding Medjugorje's messages, we find echoes of ancient truths, resonating with the sound of sacred tradition. The revelations, while private, seem to ripple outward, touching the hearts of those grounded in scripture. Could they be rooted in a deeper divine purpose, intended to guide and illuminate the paths trodden by those who seek? The convergence of doctrine, lived experience, and mystical messages formulates an epic quest for examination.

The uniqueness of Medjugorje lies in the sustained and coherent nature of the messages delivered over the decades. The Virgin Mary's words, filled with love, peace, and a call to conversion, echo biblical themes and Marian devotion, drawing parallels that reinforce their divine origin. This book places these messages within the context of sacred tradition, examining their alignment with the teachings passed through generations. In doing so, it creates a meditational framework for integrating these heavenly communications into personal prayer and reflection.

The call of Medjugorje is not limited to those inclined toward Marian devotion; it resonates with anyone who has ever sought a deeper understanding of purpose, peace, and the divine. It is an invitation to explore faith anew, to renew the spirit through prayer, fasting, and a commitment to living a life aligned with divine will. The messages encourage introspection and action, both on a personal and communal level. In embracing these practices, believers find themselves drawn into a richer, more profound union with God.

While there have been criticisms and skepticism surrounding the apparitional events in Medjugorje, their impact cannot be dismissed lightly. The phenomenon has inspired stories of conversion, peace, and miracles, personal testimonies that speak to the transformative power witnessed by countless pilgrims. It is these transformative experiences that invite a deeper investigation into the authenticity and intent of the Medjugorje messages.

Through comprehensive exploration, this book seeks to bridge the gap between faith and reason, offering insights that appeal not only to believers but to those questioning the possibility of divine intervention in the contemporary world. The aim is to provide a nuanced narrative that marries the spiritual parables of saints and philosophers, offering a textual eucharist that nourishes the soul.

As we embark on this rich journey through the layers of Medjugorje, let us approach with both fervor and an open heart. The introduction is merely the threshold to a profound exploration that seeks to deepen understanding and enrich faith through the messages delivered at this sacred site. Medjugorje beckons us all to come closer, to listen with intent, and to find meaning in its heavenly whispers.

In this space of contemplation and reflection, we are summoned to pause and consider what these messages mean for our own spiritual journeys. We ask ourselves: How do the messages of Medjugorje challenge us? Inspire us? Change us? They herald not just a return to faith but a progression toward a faith reimagined, strengthened by love and guided by divine insight.

Chapter 1: The History of Medjugorje

In June of 1981, the pastoral landscape of Medjugorje, a modest village nestled within the heart of Bosnia and Herzegovina, became hallowed ground as six young visionaries declared they had encountered the Virgin Mary. This event marked the genesis of an enduring spiritual journey that has captivated millions worldwide, igniting fervent discussion and devotion among believers. As the apparitions unfolded against the backdrop of turbulent political landscapes, they evoked parallels to biblical revelatory moments where the divine pierced through human tumult with messages of hope and repentance. The story of Medjugorje is not merely a narrative of celestial visitation but also a testament to the profound interplay between faith and culture, drawing pilgrims into a spiritual renaissance that echoes the timeless traditions of the Church. The miraculous unveilings in this rural visage invite us to ponder the intricate system of divinity interwoven throughout human history, urging a return to the core tenets of peace, prayer, and conversion.

The Origins of the Apparitions

The story of Medjugorje begins in the summer of 1981, a time when the world was wrestling with its own shadows of uncertainty and change. Nestled in the rugged hills of Bosnia and Herzegovina, the small village was far removed from the global stage. Yet, it was here that six young visionaries claimed to have encountered the Blessed Virgin Mary. This encounter was simple, profound, and marked by an otherworldly sense of peace. To understand the origins of these apparitions, one must not only look at the external circumstances but delve into the spiritual experiences woven into the hearts of these seers and the very land they walked upon.

On the seemingly ordinary day of June 24, 1981, a mystical event defied the mundane. A group of children, some friends and others siblings, ascended the stony path to Podbrdo Hill, drawn by a light that only they could perceive. It was here, amidst the stones and brush, that the Mother of God appeared to them. Though their eyes were young, their understanding was beyond their years. They described Our Lady as having a radiant beauty, standing atop a cloud, enveloped in ethereal light. It was a moment suspended in time, where heaven seemed to kiss the earth.

The apparitions initially sparked disbelief and skepticism among the villagers. It wasn't unusual, for instances of divine intervention often meet human doubt. However, those who chose to open their hearts found themselves moved by the innocence and sincerity of the seers. These children, unscathed by the complexities of adult life, were vessels of grace, encumbered only by the language of simplicity and faith.

The apparitions grew in frequency, and so did the number of those drawn to Medjugorje. The messages imparted by the Virgin Mary to the visionaries emphasized themes of peace, prayer, and conversion. Her words, like streams of living water, nourished the spiritual thirst of those who gathered. Skeptics remained, but for the devout, the hillside became a beacon of hope, a place where the veil between mortality and eternity appeared very thin indeed.

In examining the religious and historical context of the area, one can see how the apparitions fit within a larger divine narrative. The Balkans, with its intricate history of tension and faith, seemed an unlikely yet fitting stage for such heavenly visitations. It is a land of contrasts—beauty and hardship, faith and turmoil—which resonates with the biblical lands of old where prophets walked, and miracles unfolded.

Much like the origins of Christianity, the events at Medjugorje began quietly, without pomp or grandeur. Yet, the sublime nature of the novice seers' experiences carried echoes of Christ's own simple beginnings in a lowly manger, born into the world's complexity to be its peace and redemption.

The intimate relationship between the seers and Our Lady bore witness to a profound theological principle—that of God's closeness to humanity. Medjugorje became a living testament to the Catholic belief in the communion of saints, heaven's continuity with the earthly, and the embrace of the divine with human frailty. Thematic connections to Sacred Scripture became apparent; one could draw parallels with Marian appearances in the Bible, encountering the celestial through tangible, everyday means.

Reflecting on the spiritual impact of these apparitions, one could liken it to an allegorical journey of the soul. Here were young shepherds in spirit, guiding multitudes toward a renewed awareness of God's love and an invitation to live the Gospel more fully. An epiphany, mirroring the journey of the Magi, converged with Medjugorje—a star's light manifest on earth, guiding weary pilgrims toward inner transformation.

Despite the multitude of political and religious divisions present in the region, the messages of Medjugorje embraced a universal call to love and peace. Mary, as she has appeared throughout history, served as an intermediary—a bridge linking believers from various cultures and backgrounds to the singular truth of God's eternal message.

Time only solidified the stature of Medjugorje as a place of spiritual renewal. The early skeptical ambiance began to shift as stories of conversion, healing, and renewal emerged from those who made their pilgrimage to this sacred site. For many pilgrims, the journey wasn't just physical, but an inward trek toward divine reconciliation.

Engaging with the origins and unfoldment of the Medjugorje apparitions invites one to delve deeper into the notion of faith itself—a faith compounded by trust in that which is unseen, yet felt with an intensity surpassing empirical evidence. In the eyes of the faithful, these apparitions weren't just events to be witnessed but testimonies to a divine mystery unfurling in their midst.

The initial days and weeks of the apparitions concluded not with an ending, but a beginning. This event marked an ongoing spiritual saga that has drawn countless souls into its embrace. For the seekers of truth and divine encounters, Medjugorje remains a place where earth meets the luminous fringes of paradise. In understanding these origins, one grasps not just a segment of history, but the echo of an eternal call to all of mankind—an apex where the infinite reaches into the ordinary, inviting transformation.

Early Pilgrimages and Public Reaction

The once tranquil town of Medjugorje found itself at the epicenter of an extraordinary spiritual awakening when the first pilgrims arrived, drawn by whispers of divine encounters in a land marked by simplicity and grace. As news of the apparitions spread like wildfire, the pathways to this humble village were trodden by seekers of peace, yearning hearts, and curious minds alike. Through rocky terrain and under the watchful gaze of the heavens, they walked—a modern pilgrimage echoing ancient journeys to sacred sites, their souls laden with hope and silent prayers.

Those early pilgrims, much like harbingers of faith and wonder, bore witness to something that both confounded and inspired. Their numbers grew swiftly as tales of the Virgin Mary's messages and miraculous signs reached beyond borders, transcending language, and culture. These journeys were not merely physical; they evoked a profound spiritual stirring akin to the calling of the early Christians who sought truth and divine connection. It was a testament to the inherent longing for the transcendent, deeply embedded within the human spirit.

A diversity of pilgrims arrived at Medjugorje, each one carrying personal burdens and ailments, seeking solace and answers amidst the mountains. There were those afflicted by doubt, whose faith was a flickering candle struggling against the winds of modernity. Others came with steadfast certainty, eager to reinforce their beliefs through the testimonies and the palpable peace that enveloped the town. They roamed the paths where the apparitions were said to have taken place, leaving tokens of gratitude, offerings of faith, each footstep a silent testament to hope.

Public reaction to these pilgrimages was as varied and complex as humanity itself. In certain quarters, there was skepticism, a pragmatic approach questioning the fervent testimonies of those who had visited Medjugorje. Some detractors, both secular and ecclesiastical, raised concerns about the authenticity of the visions and the fervor they stirred. The Church, custodian of divine truths and doctrine, approached these claims with caution, understanding the delicate balance between sustaining the sacred and guarding against potential deception.

Amidst this swirling uncertainty, wonder persisted. Stories spread of inexplicable healings, transformations, and profound changes within those who made the journey. Eyewitness accounts painted vivid pictures of unexplainable phenomena—glimpses of light, the sun spinning in the sky, a tangible presence of peace. For many, these experiences defied rational explanation, thrusting them into the realm of the divine, where logic takes a backseat to mystery and faith flowers in the unlikeliest of conditions.

The resolve of the pilgrims was matched by their testimonies upon returning home. Communities around the globe were touched by these stories, and in small chapels and grand cathedrals alike, voices lifted in prayer for insight, for compassion, echoing the messages carried back from the heart of Bosnia and Herzegovina. Indeed, it was as though

Medjugorje had become a mirror reflecting the spiritual battles and triumphs inherent in human life, a beacon for those in search of divine guidance amid the chaos of the contemporary world.

At times, the reaction from the wider public extended beyond curiosity into the realms of fervor and devotion. For some, these pilgrimages and the resultant experiences were akin to a new Pentecost—an outpouring of the Spirit, igniting faith and fortitude in both the individual and the collective conscience. Others saw the potential for moral awakening and spiritual renewal, a clarion call to return to the roots of faith, to the virtues espoused by Christ and his followers.

As the decades progressed, the reaction didn't remain static; rather, it evolved, as did the nature of the pilgrimages themselves. What began as tentative journeys of individual exploration burgeoned into a worldwide movement, catalyzing untold gatherings and communal prayers beyond Medjugorje's boundaries. The early skepticism gave way to a tentative embrace by clergy and laypeople alike, who recognized the strength and vitality in these modern avenues of faith exploration.

This period in the history of Medjugorje is marked not just by the rally of pilgrims, but by a great dialogue within the Church and among theologians, the faithful, and those yet to find faith. It was an era of discernment, an interplay between belief and skepticism, where the mysteries of divine revelation met the analytical gaze of modernity. Nevertheless, amid all debate and discernment, the stream toward Medjugorje continued to swell, an unyielding force reflecting the inner spiritual hunger of humanity.

In summary, the early pilgrimages to Medjugorje and the global reactions they engendered reveal the profound capacity for spiritual longing and renewal. In the face of doubt, turmoil, and worldly distractions, these pilgrims and their stories highlight the sheer transformative power of hope and faith. Their journeys paved a path for a deeper understanding of divine mysteries, reminding a modern world that the search for divine truth is as old as time itself, continuing to inspire those who seek it with open hearts and minds.

Chapter 2: The Seers of Medjugorje

In the heart of the humble village of Medjugorje, nestled within the rugged embrace of Bosnia and Herzegovina, six young visionaries emerged, their lives irrevocably transformed by celestial encounters. These seers, ordinary in their daily routines, were chosen to partake in extraordinary revelations, bearing messages purportedly from the Queen of Heaven herself. Their unique journeys, marked by shared visions yet deeply personal experiences, echo with an authenticity that beckons both the faithful and the skeptical to listen with open hearts. Amidst the rolling hills and sacred silences of their village, these seers described sights of ethereal beauty, imparting words filled with hope, peace, and a divine urgency compelling the world towards spiritual awakening. Each seer, with distinct backgrounds and personalities, contributed a harmonious yet diverse testimony, as if reaffirming the manifold ways through which God's light can penetrate the human soul. This unfolding spiritual narrative, steeped in Marian devotion, invites believers to ponder the profound intricacies of faith and revelation, urging a deeper alignment with the sacred truths enshrined in Scripture and Tradition.

Personal Backgrounds of the Seers

The village of Medjugorje, nestled in the heart of Bosnia and Herzegovina, is not just a serene landscape of rolling hills and fragrant fields but also the cradle of six young souls chosen to witness the extraordinary. The seers of Medjugorje, who claimed to first encounter the Virgin Mary in 1981, came from humble beginnings, their lives reflecting the simplicity and challenges of rural life. Each seer, in their own way, embodied a unique blend of spiritual fervor and everyday humanness, making their revelations all the more compelling to both cynics and believers.

Ivan Dragicevic, born on May 25, 1965, stands out as a figure of quiet contemplation. His family was deeply rooted in the agricultural traditions of the region, and as a young boy, Ivan's routine was intertwined with the cycles of the earth. His life, steeped in prayer and labor, provided a fertile ground for the divine messages that he would later share with the world. Despite initial disbelief from some, Ivan's sincerity and unwavering faith became a cornerstone of his testimony. His encounters with the Virgin Mary were characterized by profound messages of peace and hope, resonating with the spiritual yearnings of many.

Similarly, Vicka Ivankovic-Mijatovic, born on September 3, 1964, reflected a different facet of the collective spiritual mosaic. Known for her vivacity and open heart, Vicka's experiences were marked by an exuberant connection with the divine. Raised in a family of eight children, Vicka's communal upbringing instilled in her a sense of unity and faith steadfastness. Her visions, often shared with a contagious zeal, urged individuals to embrace love and prayer. This enthusiasm didn't just illuminate the hearts of those in her immediate proximity but touched pilgrims and seekers globally.

The stories of Marija Pavlovic-Lunetti and Mirjana Dragicevic-Soldo further enrich the opus of Medjugorje's spiritual narrative. Born on April 1, 1965, Marija embraced a life illuminated by a soft but resilient faith. Her gentle nature became a vessel for messages of grace, urging conversions and inner transformations. Mirjana, on the other hand, born on March 18, 1965, brought a message of profound depth intertwined with compassion. Her annual apparitions, imbued with messages about God's love and mercy, painted a picture of divine patience and perennial hope.

Reflecting on Jakov Colo and Ivanka Ivankovic-Elez, we see the innocence and purity that underscored the divine revelations. Jakov, the youngest of the group, was just ten years old when the apparitions began. His tender age and unblemished heart perhaps made him an ideal recipient for the Virgin's messages, which emphasized a childlike trust in the divine parentage. Similarly, Ivanka was the first to witness the apparitions. Born on June 21, 1966, Ivanka experienced a narrative of personal and spiritual loss, having recently lost her mother. It was this intimate grief that the Virgin Mary addressed in their early encounters, providing a solace that transcends human comprehension.

As we stitch together their backgrounds, a vivid mural of interwoven personal and divine narrative emerges—a testament to the universality of the messages. These seers were not isolated mystics detached from reality but young villagers whose lives were fundamentally changed by their encounters. Their narratives are not just about the divine messages but also reflect a tale of living faith, a faith cultivated by experiences, doubts, and moments of profound joy and trust.

The purity of their messages and the integrity of their lives call believers to walk beside them on this journey. We are invited to explore not just their experiences but the very essence of what it means to be vessels chosen by the divine to communicate messages of eternal relevance. These seers remind us of the transformative power of faith and the enduring presence of hope and love in our midst.

As their stories unfold through the lush and sacred land of Medjugorje, we are left with a profound question—a prompt for contemplation and reflection: how do we, in our daily challenges and routines, open ourselves to the divine, allowing sacred whispers to penetrate our souls and guide our path towards spiritual fulfillment and unity? In contemplating their personal backgrounds, we are encouraged to delve deeper into the mysteries they reveal, finding inspiration in their simplicity and strength in their profound faith.

Unique Experiences of Each Seer

In the remarkable spiritual occurrences at Medjugorje, the unique experiences of each seer reveal a constellation of encounters that are both profoundly personal and enigmatically collective. These seers—visionaries who claim to have witnessed the manifestations of the Blessed Virgin Mary—bring forth narratives that, while diverse in their details, align in their ethereal essence, weaving together a fabric of divine mystery. Each seer brings a distinct perspective, akin to the varied hues in a stained-glass window, allowing the light of the divine to transcend the mundane through their unique facets.

From the outset, it was evident that the encounters of each seer were individualized, yet inexplicably unified by the overarching spiritual themes they conveyed. Take Vicka Ivanković-Mijatović, for example, whose visions often included elaborate conversations with the Virgin Mary. Vicka's experiences are marked by a vivacious energy and a profound sense of duty, her messages often encompassing not just personal revelations but expansive calls for apostolic action and global intercession. Her narratives articulate a journey of resilience, where her vibrant accounts have inspired thousands to seek solace and strength from divine sources.

Consider also the experiences of Ivan Dragicević, whose contemplative encounters present a serene contrast to Vicka's. Ivan's visions are imbued with a calmness that invites meditation and reflection, offering a gentle whisper of sacred tranquility. His profound dialogues with the apparition convey a softer, yet no less compelling, call to introspection and internal peace. The messages he has shared resonate like the gentle plucking of harp strings, each note reflective and harmonious with the larger orchestral symphony of Medjugorje's spiritual revelations.

Mirjana Dragićević-Soldo, meanwhile, has uniquely borne the weight of visions interspersed with messages that she describes as peeks into eternity. Her experiences are imbued with an acute awareness of temporality and timelessness, often revealing layers of understanding that echo prophetic tones. The emotional gravity in her accounts naturally prompts introspection on the part of the believer, inciting a deeper confrontation with the spiritual realities that transcend earthly existence. In the intersection of Mirjana's revelations and the seers' collective experiences, the faithful find avenues for personal contemplation of life's mysteries.

The youngest of the seers, Jakov Colo, provides yet another unique lens through which to view the divine encounters of Medjugorje. Jakov's visions are often couched in the innocence and pure-hearted openness of youth, tethering their weighty celestial messages with a child-like simplicity. This simplicity, however, does not dilute the profundity of his experiences but rather augments them, illustrating the core belief that faith itself is most potent when stripped of complexity and embraced with genuine sincerity. Jakov's narratives remind believers that the path to divine communion need not be arduous but can be punctuated by the sweet embrace of innocent faith.

Assuredly, Marija Pavlovic-Lunetti carries forward the experiences that further the intricate fabric of Medjugorje's revelations. Known particularly for visions that stress the importance of prayer and sacramental life, Marija articulates the efficacy of humble supplication and devotion as the stairway to heavenly accord. Her lived experiences serve as a heuristic guidepost, urging believers to cultivate prayer lives as the bedrock of faith—a theme that reverberates deeply within the spiritual messages she selflessly shares.

Ivanka Ivankovic-Elez distinguishes herself with a narrative deeply intertwined with familial connections, particularly marked by an emotionally resonant image of her deceased mother, who appears alongside the apparitions. The emotional depth of Ivanka's experiences underscores the interrelation between familial love and spiritual love, prompting believers to consider how earthly bonds may reflect divine unions. Ivanka's testimony encourages individuals to cherish relationships as sacred gifts, imbued with divine purpose and revelation.

In exploring the distinct yet harmonious experiences of these six seers, it becomes evident that their encounters form an allegorical mosaic of divine interaction with humankind, rich with spiritual veracity and faithful encouragement. Each experience is a verse in a celestial hymn, calling out to believers to partake in a symphony that spans heaven and earth. The legacy of these encounters lives on in the hearts and actions of the faithful, testifying not just to the experiences themselves but to the broader quest for transcendental truth and spiritual fulfillment. Such undeniable authenticity invites continued participation in the divine mystery encountered at Medjugorje, where the faithful can find sanctuary and strength in the unity of vision and voice.

Chapter 3: Understanding Private Revelation

To delve into the profound mystery of private revelation is to embark on a sacred journey—a journey that navigates the delicate interplay between divine communication and human reception. The Catholic Church, in her wisdom, discerns these revelations, balancing between skepticism and wonderment. Private revelations, unlike the public messages sealed within the canonical texts, whisper heaven's ongoing dialogue with the earthly realm. They emerge in a quilt of dreams, visions, and heavenly apparitions, inviting us not into new dogma, but into deeper, love-infused comprehension of eternal truths. Medjugorje stands as a luminous example: a place where revelations beckon the faithful to renew their commitment to God without veering off the well-trodden path of the Church's sacred teachings. Here, the heavenly messages offered by the seers embody a continuity with Sacred Tradition and Sacred Scripture, illustrating a divine narrative that complements rather than contradicts the foundational revelations given to humanity. We are called, therefore, to witness these revelations with the discernment of a wise scholar and the open heart of a mystic, aligning every perceived divine encounter with the timeless wisdom of our faith.

The Church's View on Private Revelation

The rich history of Catholic faith is resplendent, woven together with doctrine, scripture, and the mystical experiences known as revelations. Within this intricate design, the Church makes a critical distinction between public and private revelations. While public revelation finds its bedrock in the life and teachings of Jesus Christ, encapsulated within the canonical Bible, private revelation occurs throughout history, often through apparitions, dreams, or visions granted to individuals.

In understanding the Church's stance on private revelation, it is essential to grasp that these experiences, by themselves, do not demand the universal assent of the faithful. This is a point emphasized by the Magisterium: private revelations do not add to the deposit of faith, but they can offer guidance and encouragement for living the Gospel more fully. The role of private revelation, therefore, is not to grant new doctrines but to remind, call, and draw the faithful closer to divine truths already revealed.

The Church approaches claims of private revelation with discernment, balancing skepticism with openness to the mysteries of God. Guided by theological criteria, ecclesial investigation ensures that any new revelation harmonizes with established doctrine and fosters genuine spiritual benefit. This process entails rigorous vetting by local bishops, sustained observation, and, in some cases, judgments that can last decades or centuries. Such caution underlines the Church's commitment to safeguarding theological integrity while acknowledging the possibility of genuine divine intervention.

Consider the cautious stance taken concerning the visions at Medjugorje. Since their inception, these apparitions have captured global attention, inspiring a spectrum of opinions within the Church hierarchy and laity alike. The Church continues to study these phenomena comprehensively. With a commission established in the 2010s, its approach reflects a delicate balance: recognizing the potential for spiritual enrichment while avoiding premature validation of the messages.

Theologians remind us that, at the heart of any discernment process, lies the criterion of spiritual fruits. The authenticity of private revelation, they argue, can often be gauged by its effects—does it lead the faithful to deeper prayer, greater charity, and closer union with the Church? In the case of Medjugorje, the pilgrimages, conversions, and myriad testimonies of transformation serve as potent evidence for some of its divine origin.

Yet, the Church remains a custodian rather than a restrictor of revelation. By affirming the occasional authenticity of private revelations, as with Lourdes and Fatima, the Church keeps alive a vibrant tradition of Marian devotion. These validations are not licenses for ideological divergence but conduits for spiritual renewal, inviting the faithful to witness to the incarnational reality of God interacting with humanity.

Moreover, private revelations such as those claimed at Medjugorje often provoke theological reflection and discourse, inviting scholars to explore their alignment with

Sacred Scripture and Sacred Tradition. This ongoing examination enriches the depths of the Church's understanding of God's continuous work in the world. In discerning private revelation, the Church echoes an invitation to a deeper relationship with God through prayer and penance, mirroring the virtues championed by these divine communications.

Finally, the Church's nuanced view highlights an important pastoral approach. While the full authority of belief rests on public revelation, private revelations serve as beacons, shedding light on the path to holiness. The faithful are invited, not coerced, to embrace these messages as spiritual aids. Through them, we catch glimpses of the eternal—moments that rekindle the ageless promise of grace and glory, wrapped in the gentle veil of human vision.

Thus, while navigating the enigmatic realm of private revelations, the Church admonishes and encourages: discernment must be prayerful, guided by wisdom, and remain ever faithful to the teachings of Christ and His Church. Such is the vigilant love rooted in truth, aiming to see God's hand in the myriad experiences of the divine that fill our lives' journey.

Differentiating Private and Public Revelation

In the rich history of Catholic theology, the distinction between private and public revelation occupies a space as significant as it is nuanced. At first glance, one might assume these two forms of divine communication are but different pages from the same heavenly book. However, to comprehend them fully is to discern their distinct roles within the broader landscape of faith.

Public revelation, as associated with the Sacred Scriptures and the life of Jesus Christ, forms the bedrock of Christian belief. It is the light given once and for all, complete and sufficient for salvation. Indeed, the Church holds public revelation to be the divine message expressed through the canonical texts of the Bible, universally binding upon the faithful. Each word and passage is considered the inspired Word of God, encompassing the divine plan from Genesis to the Apocalypse. In essence, public revelation carries with it an authoritative weight, requiring the assent of every believer.

In contrast, private revelation emerges as a more intimate whisper, tailored not for the universal Church but for individuals and communities at specific moments in time. As described by the Congregation for the Doctrine of the Faith, private revelations may offer guidance, encouragement, or warning, but they do not add to the deposit of faith. Instead, they illuminate pathways already charted by the Scriptures, allowing for a deeper personal encounter with the divine.

The apparitions of Medjugorje, therefore, stand within this realm of private revelation. They invite those who are attentive to hear a resonant echo of the celestial realm, one that aligns with and enriches the truths already revealed. The Virgin Mary's messages there— whether advocating for peace, urging conversion, or encouraging prayer—do not replace the Gospel but rather re-present it in vibrant, accessible forms. For the pilgrims who journey to Medjugorje, these messages have kindled fires of faith, transforming everyday lives into profound testimonials of divine love.

Yet, the Church approaches private revelations with careful discernment, seeking harmony between the messages received and the truths upheld by tradition. This discernment ensures that no private revelation contradicts or replaces the core teachings of the faith. The Church, with her wisdom and prudence, acts as the guardian of this distinction, continuously evaluating such revelations to ensure they align with the deposit of faith and serve the spiritual welfare of the faithful.

It is important to recognize that the acceptance of private revelation remains optional, not a doctrinal requirement. Unlike public revelation, which demands the full assent of faith, private revelation is accepted with what is known as "ecclesiastical faith". This means believers are invited to hold these revelations with reverential confidence, should they prove consistent with Christian doctrine and bear spiritual fruit. The dynamic between assent and personal discernment exemplifies the Church's openness to the diverse ways in which God continues to interact with humanity.

The messages at Medjugorje echo this sentiment by inviting believers into a contemplative journey. They call the faithful to engage with ancient truths through a modern lens, where one may find encouragement and challenges alike. For those responsive to these private revelations, the messages act as spiritual compasses, guiding their hearts toward the ultimate truth found in Christ and His Church.

Understanding this dichotomy, therefore, is not merely an academic exercise but an invitation to a deeper relationship with the divine. It encourages each believer to approach both types of revelation with a spirit of discernment, recognizing the profound interplay between personal encounters and the established tenets of faith. In doing so, Catholics are empowered to live out their spiritual lives with authenticity and depth, always aligned with the broader ecclesial community.

This distinction also encourages further exploration and appreciation of how God communicates in nuanced and transformative ways. Through prayerful reflection and theological study, believers can develop a holistic understanding of revelation. This holistic grasp is not static but dynamically interacts with the living tradition of the Church, safeguarding the faith while allowing for the fresh expressions of divine love seen in private revelations like those in Medjugorje.

As we embark on the journey through this book, reflecting on the revelations of Medjugorje, let this understanding of private revelation serve as a foundational guide. By appreciating its place within the wider context of public revelation, readers may better discern the celestial messages that beckon from Bosnia-Herzegovina, nurturing hearts and souls thirsty for divine truth. In this sacred endeavor, we don't merely listen—we encounter, we discern, and through the gift of revelation, we seek the same transformative grace bestowed upon those six young seers from Medjugorje.

Chapter 4: Biblical Revelations and Medjugorje

In the mysterious interplay between divine revelations and the sacred sites of Medjugorje, a profound system unfolds, drawing intricate connections to the stories and prophecies etched in the Bible. As seers recount their heavenly visions, we are compelled to ponder parallels with the Old and New Testament revelations, where the profound themes of repentance, hope, and divine love reside. These apparitions, set against the backdrop of age-old biblical traditions, invite us to see Medjugorje not as a new narrative, but one deeply woven into the eternal scripture. Like the prophets of ancient times, the seers shine a light on the timeless pursuit of understanding God's will, urging us closer to the heart of faith. This chapter seeks to uncover how these modern visions breathe life into biblical allegories and reinforce the sacred path laid through the annals of spiritual history, awakening hearts to the celestial echoes of a divinely inspired journey.

Connections to Old Testament Themes

The visions and messages experienced by the seers of Medjugorje resonate deeply with the themes that run through the Old Testament, creating a rich construct of continuity and renewal in divine communication. The Old Testament is a sprawling narrative of God's engagement with humanity, filled with stories of prophecy, revelation, and divine law. In comparing these ancient scriptures with the modern experiences of Medjugorje, we uncover echoes of divine consistency, reinforcing that the messages received by the seers are both timeless and rooted in Sacred Tradition.

To begin with, one can draw a parallel between the prophetic nature of the messages in Medjugorje and the Old Testament prophets. Figures such as Isaiah, Jeremiah, and Ezekiel were not merely messengers but were also vessels of divine admonishment and hope. Just as these prophets called Israel to repentance and renewal, advocating for a return to the covenant with God, the messages from Medjugorje emphasize themes of conversion, repentance, and spiritual awakening. This continuity suggests that God's desire for a deep, transformative relationship with His people is an enduring theme, transcending time and space.

Moreover, the messages of Medjugorje often remind us of the covenant relationship, a cornerstone in Old Testament theology. The covenant established with Abraham, and later renewed with Moses and David, highlights God's steadfast promise and faithfulness. The Medjugorje messages often call people back to their covenantal commitments—their baptismal promises—and encourage a life aligned with divine will. This dynamic recalls the cycles in the Old Testament where the Israelites returned to God's covenant through renewed faith and obedience.

These messages also echo the wisdom literature of the Old Testament, such as Proverbs and Ecclesiastes, where the pursuit of wisdom and understanding is framed as a spiritual journey. The Medjugorje apparitions encourage a life imbued with wisdom drawn from prayer, reflection, and discernment. Similarly, the quest for divine wisdom is not merely intellectual but transformative, shaping one's heart and actions toward holiness and virtue.

The narrative of Medjugorje can also be seen in the light of the Exodus story, where liberation leads to a new path of transformation. The Israelites' journey from slavery in Egypt to the Promised Land is symbolic of spiritual liberation. Medjugorje calls those who listen to its messages to embark on their personal exodus—from the bondage of sin and spiritual apathy to the freedom of divine grace and joyful living in God's presence.

Notably, the visions of Medjugorje evoke the image of the Old Testament altar, where encounters and covenants with God were often reaffirmed. Altars were places of sacrifice, worship, and communication with the divine—an echo resounds in the way Medjugorje becomes a spiritual altar for those seeking divine connection and grace through prayer and communal experiences.

The Medjugorje messages also emphasize peace, echoing the prophetic vision of the messianic age found in texts like Isaiah, where swords turn to plowshares, and peace reigns. The Old Testament foretold a time of divine peace that should embrace the world, and in Medjugorje, we find an invitation to become instruments of this peace in a troubled world, heralding a new era of reconciliation and hope.

Another meaningful connection arises in the area of divine supplication and intercession, themes richly woven throughout Psalms and prophetic literature. The apparitions' call for prayer reflects the Old Testament's persistent theme that humans are to engage in constant dialogue with God. The laments, thanksgivings, and supplications of the Psalms find their echo in Medjugorje's encouragement to seek intimacy with God through heartfelt prayer and to make intercession a daily practice.

Lastly, one cannot overlook the connection to the prophetic imagery often deployed in both the Old Testament and Medjugorje experiences. The use of visions, signs, and symbolic language in scriptures like Daniel and Ezekiel are tools for conveying God's message to His people. Medjugorje's visionary experiences, rich in symbolic meaning and allegory, serve to capture the attention and elevate the spiritual understanding of those who encounter them.

In reflecting upon these connections, you see how the messages of Medjugorje extend the unbroken line of divine revelation seen in the Old Testament, further underscoring the consistency of God's message throughout time. These reflections bolster the conviction that the apparitions are heavenly in origin, aligning seamlessly with the foundational tenets of Sacred Scripture, and continue to guide those who seek God's truth into a fuller understanding and richer relationship with the divine. Medjugorje, with its profound connections to age-old themes, becomes a place of spiritual pilgrimage where the whispers of ancient scripture meet the heart's yearning for contemporary understanding and grace.

New Testament Parallels

In the lush fields of theological discourse, the visions at Medjugorje weave themselves into the tapestry of New Testament narratives with an intricate complexity that beckons careful exploration. It's as though the whispers of ancient witnesses have traveled through the annals of time, converging upon a modern tableau of spiritual revelation. Those familiar with the Medjugorje apparitions will recognize the echoes of an earlier covenant, one borne from the pages of the New Testament and brought alive through the seers' experiences.

Draw parallels to the most famous New Testament account: the Annunciation. Here, we see an angelic visitation to Mary, a young girl from Nazareth chosen to bear the Son of God. In Medjugorje, too, we witness visitations—profound and transformative. These encounters underscore the enduring relevance of Marian interventions, reminiscent of the moment the Angel Gabriel declared, "Hail, full of grace." The seers, much like Mary, find themselves in awe, fear, and then acceptance of the divine message. They remind us of the humble acceptance and profound responsibility that come with receiving such celestial communication.

The Beatitudes, part of Jesus's Sermon on the Mount, further find their reflection in Medjugorje's messages. The call to be "poor in spirit" echoes in the invitation to humility and the encouragement to lead a life imbued with grace and simplicity. A deep yearning for peace resonates through these messages, much as Jesus proclaimed, "Blessed are the peacemakers, for they shall be called the children of God." Medjugorje's emphasis on peace emerges not as a mere absence of conflict but as an active state of tranquility, derived from divine harmony and inner serenity. The seers become vessels of this promise, carrying forth a vision of beatific peace.

Consider the Eucharistic imagery prevalent throughout the New Testament, showcasing elements of sacrifice, communion, and transformation. Medjugorje's messages often return to these themes, urging the faithful to partake in the sacraments with reverence and regularity. In the way the Last Supper invites us into communion with the divine, Medjugorje reminds us of the living presence of Christ in our everyday lives. The allegorical significance transcends ritual and calls us to embrace a life united with the Holy Spirit, just as the disciples were invited to dwell in unity with Christ.

The transformative journey of St. Paul offers another rich parallel. Once a persecutor of Christians, his road to Damascus encounter became a moment of radical conversion. The messages from Medjugorje consistently advocate for personal conversion, inviting the faithful to turn away from sin and embrace a renewed life in Christ. Each apparition acts as a spiritual Damascus, challenging individuals to confront their own paths and consider profound changes that align with God's intentions.

Moreover, the Acts of the Apostles describe the early Christian community's life, marked by prayer, sharing, and fellowship. The manifestations at Medjugorje similarly call for a return to daily prayer, communal worship, and shared spiritual growth. They resonate with the early Church's spirit, cultivating a sense of unity among believers and fostering a community that supports each other in faith and practice.

Christ's parables, rich with allegory and moral instruction, appear mirrored in the Medjugorje messages, which often employ simple, relatable language to convey profound spiritual truths. Like the Parable of the Sower, these messages challenge us to examine the soil of our hearts—whether we are receptive or resistant to the divine word, whether the seeds of faith can flourish within us amidst trials and distractions.

In reflecting on the story of the Transfiguration, where Christ's divine glory is revealed to Peter, James, and John, we find a connection with the Medjugorje narrative. Here, the supernatural experiences of the seers, though fleeting and enigmatic, offer a glimpse into heaven's splendor. They serve as reminders of the luminous presence of God's kingdom, intertwined with our earthly existence—a prefiguration of eternal bliss.

As we navigate through the pages of the New Testament and the unfolding story of Medjugorje, the parallels become unmistakable expressions of divine love and mercy. They call out to each believer, inviting a deeper exploration of faith and a more profound commitment to living out the Gospel. These revelations, like the scriptures, become a compass, guiding us towards spiritual enlightenment and the promise of salvation.

In this grand narrative arc, not only do the events of Medjugorje find resonance with the sacred texts of old, but they also breathe anew the timeless truths that persist through generations. Through these parallels, we are drawn to consider the unfolding mystery of our own faith journeys, inspired to live each day in harmony with the messages that echo throughout the sacred spaces of past and present.

Chapter 5: Messages of Hope

In the heart of Medjugorje's messages lies an unwavering assurance of hope that resonates deeply with the faithful, offering a bridge between the celestial and the terrestrial. This divine beacon illuminates the path of the weary and the burdened, urging believers to embrace a future woven with divine promise. The Blessed Mother's words gently entwine with the Scriptures, painting an allegory of endless hope grounded in love and redemption. Pilgrims recount transformative encounters—a testament to the profound efficacy of these heavenly whispers—experiencing renewal where despair once loomed. Each message is a clarion call, both an epic and intimate reflection of God's everlasting mercy, inspiring a vibrant and unwavering faith that transcends the trials of earthly existence. Hope, thus delivered, becomes not just a virtue but a lived experience, inviting all to partake in the eternal promise of divine grace.

Common Themes in the Messages

Throughout the unfolding story of Medjugorje, certain recurring messages have resonated with pilgrims and believers alike, coalescing varying themes that point towards spiritual renewal and divine guidance. Central to these messages is the call to deepen one's faith, embody a life of prayer, and commit to personal transformation. These messages, often perceived as heavenly whispers, are not mere echoes from a distant realm but resounding invitations to walk a path of sanctity and devotion.

One of the most profound themes is the invitation to prayer, echoing a drumbeat that reverberates throughout the stories and experiences shared by those who have heeded the call. Prayer is presented not simply as a ritual, but as an intimate dialogue with the Divine, a lifeline that nourishes the soul and anchors the believer amidst life's tempests. The emphasis on daily prayer, especially the Rosary, reflects a profound connection to tradition, urging the faithful to draw nearer to the heart of Mary and, through her, to the mysteries of Christ.

A closely linked theme is the call for peace. The messages of Medjugorje emphasize inner and outer peace, suggesting that transformation begins within oneself before radiating outward to heal communities and, ultimately, the world. This peace is not a serene absence of conflict but a dynamic state achieved through reconciliation with God and with others, mirroring the beatitudes and teachings of Christ that call for peacemaking as a blessed vocation.

Accompanying the call to prayer and peace is a persistent exhortation toward fasting and repentance. The messages often convey that fasting is not merely abstention but a means to purify the heart, clear the mind, and foster a spirit of humility. It is portrayed as a tangible expression of contrition and a powerful tool for spiritual warfare, echoing scriptural teachings that depict fasting as integral to dismantling spiritual strongholds and opening avenues of grace.

Alongside these practices arises a theme of conversion, urging individuals to turn away from sinful paths and embrace a renewed life in Christ. Conversion, as expressed in these messages, is not a one-time event but a continual process of shedding old ways and habits in pursuit of virtue and divine intimacy. It is a radical reorientation of one's life direction, aligning one's will with God's, illustrating the perennial patience and grace of divine love that awaits every willing heart.

Further reinforcing these stalwart themes are messages of hope and love. Medjugorje fosters an enduring hope that pervades even the darkest hours, reminding believers that they are enveloped in a love that exceeds all understanding. This hope is intertwined with an acknowledgment of life's trials yet insists that through faith and perseverance, one can overcome any adversity.

The messages also repeatedly stress the importance of community and living out one's faith as a testimony to others. This manifests in active love and service, encouraging believers to become vessels of God's love in the world, living exemplars of gospel values. It aligns with the Church's teaching of faith as both personal and communal, where believers gather as the body of Christ to worship, support, and spur one another on in their spiritual journeys.

These themes, while individually significant, converge to form a holistic vision of a life led by divine guidance and filled with purpose. The messages of Medjugorje, while deeply rooted in Catholic tradition, transcend religious boundaries, offering universal truths that speak to the human condition. They remind us that a transformative relationship with the divine is both possible and necessary.

Ultimately, the messages' consistent themes encourage a return to simplicity, inviting believers to strip away the complexities of modern life and rediscover the simplicities of faith—trust, surrender, love, and service. In this return, there lies the promise of a restored world, reflecting the gentle and persistent promise that echoes through the sacred folds of time: with God, all things are possible.

Transformational Stories from Pilgrims

Perhaps it is in the simple stories of individual lives profoundly changed that we glimpse the essence of hope intertwined with the divine. Medjugorje, a place where heaven seems to touch the earth, offers countless testimonies of transformation that tug at the heartstrings of our faith. In these hills swept by winds of spirituality, pilgrims have found solace, conversion, and profound alteration of their soul's journey. Let's delve into these stories, tales that remind us of the unwavering hope and the celestial whispers that beckon us to look beyond the veil of the everyday.

Consider the tale of Maria, a woman tormented by despair, having lost her way amidst life's myriad challenges. Her pilgrimage to Medjugorje wasn't driven by a firm belief but rather a last-ditch plea for help. She described her arrival as stepping into a realm of inexplicable peace. Participating in the meditative silences and communal prayers, she felt an overwhelming sense of being cradled by a loving presence. It was here in this sacred sanctuary that Maria experienced a reawakening of sorts—her heart, once heavy with sorrow, began to blossom with hope. She returned home not entirely devoid of life's difficulties but definitely equipped with an armor of faith and grace, renewed by a conviction that her journey was shared with a celestial companion.

An equally moving story is that of Jacob, a man whose faith had grown tepid over the years. His pilgrimage was an exploratory quest prompted by nudges from family and friends. Initially skeptical, Jacob found his defenses slowly dismantled. Witnessing the fervor of others and walking the paths that the seers had trodden, he was drawn into the profound simplicity of prayer and surrender. Jacob spoke of a particular moment during evening adoration where time seemed to halt. A profound silence took hold, not just around him but within him. In that moment, he encountered what felt like the very presence of Our Lady, a maternal assurance that called him back to the heart of faith he had once cherished. His life post-pilgrimage became a testament to this rekindled spirit, embracing a more active and joyful participation in both his family and community.

These stories, filled with both quiet moments of inner joy and public affirmations of faith, are not rare but rather abundant among the many who have journeyed to Medjugorje. People speak of healing and transformation, not just on an individual level but also communal. It is not uncommon to hear of families brought closer, of friendships deepened, and communities invigorated by the shared experience of a pilgrimage filled with grace and introspection.

We must also acknowledge the story of Sarah, a young mother who counts her Medjugorje pilgrimage as the cornerstone of her spiritual life. Her life was shadowed by a battle with addiction, leaving a trail of broken relationships and lost opportunities. Her decision to visit Medjugorje was born from a conversation with an old friend, herself a beneficiary of the place's transformative spiritual ambiance. Sarah recounts her transformative moment during a communal recitation of the rosary on Apparition Hill. For her, it was as if the weight of doubt and fear was lifted, replaced by an overwhelming sense of love that enveloped her wholly. This experience marked the beginning of her recovery, a turn towards a life renewed, guided by the messages of hope and continuous personal conversion.

The narratives from Medjugorje also echo tales of healing in other forms—body, mind, and soul. Anna's narrative exemplifies this, where words seem inadequate to fully capture the mystery of divine intervention. Suffering from a long-term illness, her pilgrimage wasn't about seeking a miracle but finding peace. Yet, against all odds, she experienced a profound improvement in her physical state, which her doctors had considered unlikely. She attributes her well-being not solely to the physical healing but to the spiritual completeness she felt enshrined by her pilgrimage experience. For Anna, it was an act of grace that not only renewed her body but expanded her heart with gratitude and purpose.

It is said that faith gives us the eyes to see beyond the obvious, to perceive the intertwining of divine will in our daily lives. The pilgrim's path at Medjugorje offers a unique canvas upon which these stories of transformation are painted. Each tale contributes to a broader mosaic of living testimonies, where hearts unveil their deepest longing for meaning and redemption. These are not just stories but living affirmations of the messages of hope that Medjugorje unfurls to the world.

Listening to the accounts from Medjugorje, patterns emerge—mirrors of the scriptural invitations to faith and surrender. These stories speak of the mystical intersections between heaven's whispers and earthly life's ebbs and flows. They call us to ponder our own journeys and the divine touch that seeks residence in every human heart. Through the experiences of the pilgrims, we are beckoned to embrace the possibility of our stories being touched by the same transformative grace.

Ultimately, these tales are more than mere anecdotes; they are spiritual landmarks that inspire and challenge us. They invite us into a deeper understanding of prayer, reflection, and above all, hope. For those steadfast in their faith, and for those who find themselves lost, these transformational stories from Medjugorje become lighthouses guiding humanity back to the heart of love found in the sacred messages of Medjugorje—a beacon of hope that resonates with anyone willing to listen.

Chapter 6: Messages of Peace

As the gentle whispers of Medjugorje echo through the hearts of the faithful, the call to embrace a profound peace resonates deeply with every soul willing to listen. The messages received by the seers unfurl as a sacred scroll, inviting believers to introduce peace into the essence of their daily lives, transcending the tumultuous tides of the world. Imbued with celestial wisdom, these divine communications urge a transformation that begins within, fostering a spirit of reconciliation and love that radiates outward, touching communities and nations alike. In an allegorical dance between heaven and earth, the apparitions present peace not merely as an absence of conflict but as a presence of justice, a harmony that aligns with the eternal principles of Sacred Tradition and Sacred Scripture. Herein lies a clarion invitation—an opportunity to embark on an epic journey toward a serene and divine tranquility, sculpting a world where peace reigns not just as a distant ideal but as a living, breathing reality.

The Call to Peace in Medjugorje

The message of peace resounds through the hills and churches of Medjugorje like an ancient hymn that echoes across time and space. It is a refrain tempering hearts, calling the faithful to listen with greater attentiveness, urging us to transform our conflicts into communion. Such is the profound call of the apparitions in Medjugorje—a call that shakes the dust from our souls, reminding us of our own sacred duty to be peacemakers in a world thirsting for this elusive grace.

As the apparitions progressed, a remarkable repository of divine wisdom began to emerge, one that bears the unmistakable imprint of heaven. Within these messages, peace is not merely an abstract ideal but an essential reality that must be cultivated and embodied. Our Lady's exhortation pierces through the noise of a divided planet, inviting each of us to step into the unfolding of God's restorative plan. Peace, in this context, transcends political agendas and embraces the personal; it requires a profound inner transformation, beckoning us to align our hearts with the Savior's message of love and unity.

We find in these heavenly missives a connection that bridges the temporal with the eternal. They remind us that the pursuit of peace is both an individual and communal journey. It necessitates that we not only seek solace for our own spirits but that we also actively foster harmony within our families, communities, and beyond. Our Lady's vision, as revealed to the seers, is one of comprehensive reconciliation, a call to which our very souls must respond.

The narrative of Medjugorje is steeped in a profound biblical resonance. Just as Christ took to the Mount of Olives, proclaiming peace amidst impending turmoil, so too do the seers convey a similar message on behalf of the Blessed Virgin, urging humanity toward a more divine path of peace. This resonance reminds us that biblical peace, or "shalom," is a completeness, a wholeness that encompasses justice and righteousness. Such was the vision of the prophets, and it is the same vision reawakened through the apparitions in Medjugorje.

In examining these messages, we note that they have been shared at a time in history when division feels insurmountable, and the clamor of unrest is deafening. Our Lady's call to peace doesn't demand immediate change, but rather, gradual transformation. For the people willing to embark upon this spiritual journey, it's essential to discern how true peace is cultivated—through prayer, sacrifice, and sincere acts of love.

Ultimately, the Medjugorje apparitions underscore a truth that is humbling in its simplicity yet overwhelmingly profound: lasting peace begins within the human heart. This is a peace that transcends differences and overcomes enmity, a divine invitation to lay down our grievances and lift up our shared humanity. It is an exhortation to live in accord with the Gospel, embracing the radical peace Christ extends to us through a life devoted to compassion, understanding, and forgiveness.

To those who encounter the messages of Medjugorje, there is an imperative to become apostles of peace. This is a transformative commission, inviting us to take an active stance—not only to live in peace but to become advocates and practitioners of this blessed state. Blessed are the peacemakers, and blessed indeed are those who answer this call, for they will find themselves united into the larger construct of God's divine harmony.

There's a deep allegory in the simplicity of these messages, akin to the parables of Christ. Their apparent simplicity hides a complex experience that touches both individuals and the collective body of the faithful. Each message is a mosaic tile in the larger portrait of spiritual transformation. We are called not just to see with our eyes but to perceive with the heart, to understand that the peace of Medjugorje is a spiritual discipline that encompasses patience, persistence, and boundless love.

The journey towards peace requires embracing a state of grace where we ceaselessly pray for the world's healing amid its many wounds. Medjugorje's messages offer a divine roadmap. They provide a path that winds through forgiveness and understanding, ending with the profound realization that our individual actions ripple far beyond our immediate sphere, touching souls we may not even know.

The call to peace in Medjugorje echoes the heart's deepest yearning and challenges us to become leaders in this divine pilgrimage. The apparitions are a guiding light, illuminating a path that transcends earthly turmoil, pointing us to that heavenly home where peace reigns eternal. In embracing this call, we align ourselves with the sacred rhythm of creation, and in doing so, we find consolation, purpose, and a profound sense of divine love invigorating our journey.

In this call, the seers convey not only the words of Our Lady but also her intense sorrow for the world's suffering. To respond to this plea is to answer a mother's cry for her children's unity. It is to declare, through our actions and prayers, our commitment to building a kingdom on earth that reflects the heavenly peace we yearn to share. It is, in essence, a covenant with the Creator to be instruments of His peace, healers of divisions, and harbingers of hope.

Thus, the call to peace in Medjugorje is more than a message; it is a divine injunction inviting us to actively participate in the beauty of creation as envisioned by God. All who heed the call become co-creators, charged with the sacred duty to nurture peace, both within and without. In this sacred task, we find our fuller selves, living testimonies to the love and grace gifted from Heaven above, urging a broken world towards wholeness, and reminding it of the profound peace that resides at the heart of all things.

World Peace and Personal Transformation

In the gentle valleys of Medjugorje, where the sacred and the earthly meet in whispers of divine echoes, the call for world peace resonates with an urgency that transcends time and place. Here, amidst the serenity of this quiet village, messages that stir the soul implore humanity to weave peace not only into the fabric of nations but also into the very essence of personal transformation.

The pleas of Medjugorje are not just idyllic musings; they are a solemn reminder of our collective responsibility. Peace in the world, it seems, is inseparable from peace within the heart. This realization, rooted in the heart of these sacred apparitions, becomes an invitation—a gentle yet profound beckoning toward introspection and change.

Understanding world peace as an outflow of personal transformation may seem an immense task. Yet, the visions shared at Medjugorje insist that it is within reach. By first seeking peace in our own hearts through prayer, reflection, and the humble acceptance of divine love, we lay the groundwork for a global transformation. This is a journey where personal conversion becomes the spark for communal harmony.

As pilgrims have discovered, these messages align closely with biblical teachings, echoing the mandate of Christ to "love thy neighbor as thyself." In seeking personal peace, we mirror that ancient prayer for a world where swords are turned into plowshares, where reconciliation replaces conflict. The path of peace calls for an awakening that begins in the silence of our soul, nurtured by divine grace and unwavering hope.

The transformative power of peace is evident in the stories of those who have ventured to Medjugorje. Many arrive burdened with personal struggles—internal wars that have scarred their spirits. Yet, in the embrace of this sacred place, they find renewal, emerging as beacons of peace. This metamorphosis is neither magic nor merely emotional; it is a profound rebirth, grounded in spiritual awakening and repentance.

In the deposit of Sacred Scripture, themes of peace are woven throughout, offering countless illustrations of how personal change fosters communal peace. From the Psalms, where the Psalmist cries out for peace within his walls, to the Beatitudes, which praise peacemakers as blessed, the messages of Medjugorje find a strong foundation. They renew our understanding of peace as a dynamic force, a living testament to God's promise of salvation and harmony.

The unique experiences of the Medjugorje seers provide us with a roadmap for this transformation. Through their own journeys, they have become living examples of how personal encounters with the divine can catalyze profound change. These seers, touched by celestial visions, remind us that authentic peace requires a profound receptivity to God's will, a willingness to act with courage and humility.

Indeed, the epic journey toward peace begins with listening. In his philosophical musings, Thomas Aquinas expounded upon the role of divine wisdom in shaping moral actions, and so too do the messages of Medjugorje urge us to attune our ears to heavenly guidance. In listening, we lay the groundwork for a transformation that blossoms first within, then extends outward to the wider world.

This individual journey toward peace is far from a solitary endeavor. It becomes a shared pilgrimage—a communal walk towards unity that strengthens the bonds of Christian fellowship. In these trials and triumphs, each transformed heart becomes a testimony to the power of divine love to subdue the chaos of a broken world.

As we tread upon this path, the influence of personal transformation radiates outward, inspiring change that defies worldly expectations. It is as if each individual's conversion plants seeds of peace that grow within families, communities, and nations. Medjugorje challenges us to imagine this world—one where the pursuit of peace is relentless and transformative for all creation.

The allegorical richness of these messages beckons us to consider the broader implications of peace and transformation. Like the parables of old, Medjugorje's call leads us to contemplate what it means to be agents of peace amid discord, as seekers of light amidst shadows. The visions implore us to rise above our divided world and become artisans of unity as heralds of a future rooted not in division, but in divine fellowship.

So, as these reflections unfold, they urge us to actively engage with the messages of Medjugorje. Let them stir within us a desire for a peace that passes all understanding, a journey of transformation that begins with the profound reconciliation of our own hearts. Through this, we become co-creators of a world aligned with God's vision—a world where peace is both our starting point and our ultimate destination.

Chapter 7: Messages of Prayer

In the valley of Medjugorje, where the humble whispers of faith echo through the mountains, the call to prayer resonates as a sacred symphony manifesting the divine plea for a deeper communion with God. The apparitions convey an urgent and tender invitation to embrace daily prayer practices, weaving them into the fabric of one's quotidian journey. It's whispered through the seers that each Hail Mary in the Rosary is a spiritual balm, tending to the wounds of a world in need of healing and peace. With an urgency akin to the ancient prophets, the messages of prayer stir a renewal akin to the Pentecostal flame, igniting hearts towards holiness and rekindling the soul's devotion. Grounded in the rich soil of Sacred Tradition and Scripture, this celestial beckoning harmonizes with Christ's eternal invitation to abide in Him, offering a pathway to enlightenment as profound and mysterious as heaven's own veil. Each robed figure in this sacred drama, from the Mother of God to the local villagers, becomes an allegory, teaching that even the simplest prayer, spoken with sincerity, fashions a bridge between the temporal and the eternal, casting open the divine embrace. Through this prayerful dialogue, believers find themselves not only understood but loved beyond measure, called to carry this luminous message into the heart of the Church and world.

Encouragement of Daily Prayer Practices

In the sacred apparitions of Medjugorje, prayer is the golden experience embedded through the messages of Our Lady. It is a call to commune with the divine each day, a summons whispered like a gentle breeze through the heart of humanity. The significance of daily prayer cannot be overstated. It is in these quiet moments of devotion that one's spirit finds solace, and it is through prayer that we align ourselves with the heavenly mysteries revealed to the seers. The daily act of prayer uplifts the soul and beckons each believer toward a deeper union with God, creating a bond that is both timeless and eternally renewing.

When contemplating the encouragement for daily prayer, it's captivating to consider that Medjugorje's messages urge believers to view prayer as an indispensable part of daily life. Rather than treating prayer as a duty bound by obligation, the visionaries present it as a joyful offering, a sacred conversation with the Divine. Prayer, in this context, transcends mere words; it becomes a living dialogue that pulses with life and grace. It takes on a rhythm akin to the heartbeat—constant, reassuring, and essential for spiritual vitality.

One cannot ignore the epic nature of this call, akin to a summons from a mythic saga, drawing believers into a narrative woven with cosmic significance. The encouragement to engage with prayer daily is reminiscent of a hero journey, where the soul embarks on quests of introspection and divine discovery. These prayers form a bridge that spans the temporal and the eternal, inviting each participant into a mystical dance with the Creator.

The messages conveyed through the Medjugorje apparitions interlace prayer with purpose, guiding believers into a deeper understanding of their faith. In a world where distractions abound, daily prayer serves as a compass, keeping individuals aligned with the truth and beauty of their spiritual path. This call to prayer inspires perseverance and fortitude, echoing the virtues championed by saints and scholars throughout Catholic tradition.

Incorporating daily prayer into one's routine is an act of faith as well as discipline. It's an open door to grace, requiring a conscious decision to step through with humility and sincerity. The rhythm of prayer can take many forms, from the quiet contemplation of the heart to the recitation of the Rosary. Regardless of the method, what's essential is the constancy and commitment to engage with God each day. Herein lies the allegorical journey—the soul's pilgrimage toward divine intimacy.

Medjugorje's visionaries emphasize the transformative power of prayer. This practice fosters inner peace, healing the fractures within the human soul and sparking a cascade of spiritual renewal. Through daily prayer, believers tap into a source of light that dispels the shadows of doubt and fear. Just as the sun rises to chase away the night, prayer illuminates the spirit, casting aside darkness to reveal the radiant truth of God's love.

The simplicity of a daily prayer routine can sometimes belie its profound impact. As you immerse yourself in the practice, you find a natural ebb and flow—a connection to the liturgical calendar, a movement through the seasons of the soul. This daily commitment becomes a steady tide, carving out a sacred space within your life where divine grace can flourish. It is a nurturing ground for virtues to grow, for patience, wisdom, and compassion to take root and blossom.

Psychologists might call it ritual; theologians, sanctification. Whatever the name, the effect is undeniable. The act of returning to prayer each day brings one into a divine embrace, a safe harbor in the tumultuous sea of life. It nourishes the spirit like bread satisfies hunger, unlocking reservoirs of strength and courage needed to navigate life's challenges.

In the allegory of Medjugorje, prayer is portrayed not just as a personal endeavor but a communal one. It binds the faithful together in a spiritual kinship that transcends geographical boundaries and cultural divides. As pilgrims and believers worldwide join their voices in prayer—whether in homes, churches, or distant lands—they become part of a universal chorus, resonating with the heartbeat of heaven. Such is the power of prayer to unite and to heal, reflecting the profound interconnectedness of the human family under God's watchful care.

Regarding the seers' encouragement for daily prayer, we see a reflection of the Catholic Church's teachings—a living testament to the importance of prayer in spiritual growth and discernment. The messages affirm the richness found within the tradition of prayer, echoing the Church's wisdom through the ages. They call believers to enter into the rhythm of prayer with the trust of a child, the courage of a martyr, and the love of a mystic.

To engage in daily prayer is to participate in a legacy that stretches back through the annals of time, across the sacred pages of history. It is a call to persist in a pursuit of holiness and divine intimacy, a journey that begins anew with each whispered "Amen." In this sacred practice, the visions of Medjugorje offer light and guidance, a celestial beacon pointing the way to divine encounters and eternal truths.

Through prayer, the messages of Medjugorje plant seeds of hope and transformation, inviting believers to cultivate this garden of grace daily. It is through this practice that hearts are transformed, lives are renewed, and the soul finds its true home in the heart of the Divine, which is the ultimate destination of our prayers and our pilgrimage.

The Role of the Rosary

In the serene embrace of Medjugorje, where the sacred and the earthly intertwine, the Rosary emerges as a beacon of contemplation and divine connection. This humble chain of beads transcends the simple act of prayer into a profound journey, ushering souls into a rhythm that echoes the heartbeats of Heaven. As Our Lady of Medjugorje herself has often imparted, the Rosary is not merely a prayer but an invitation—a call to immerse oneself in the divine mysteries and to walk the path of grace and peace.

The Rosary, with its ancient roots and rich tradition, holds a cherished place within the Catholic faith. It acts as a tangible link to a spiritual heritage that has sustained believers for centuries, offering a structured yet deeply personal form of communion with God. In Medjugorje, the Rosary takes on new dimensions of significance. The messages of the visionaries affirm its power, not just as a tool for personal reflection, but as a conduit through which divine messages are received and understood in the context of our modern lives.

Vividly colored by the apparitions of the Blessed Virgin Mary, the Rosary in Medjugorje captivates the faithful with its promise of spiritual renewal and transformation. These messages beckon believers to embrace the Rosary as a shield of protection, a beacon of hope, and a bridge to deeper spiritual truths. It is through the Rosary that many have found solace, guidance, and an amplified sense of purpose in their spiritual journey.

Our Lady's repeated emphasis on the Rosary in her messages serves as a reminder of its potency. The Rosary becomes a melodious prayer that reaches the deepest corners of the soul, aligning the heartbeat with the rhythm of divine love. Each decade is a step forward, a sequence in the heavenly dance that connects human frailty with celestial strength, highlighting moments in the life of Christ and the Virgin Mary.

The true power of the Rosary lies not only in its recitation but also in its meditation. Each mystery opens a window into a Gospel scene, allowing the faithful to ponder the divine mysteries anew. This rhythmic contemplation leads the soul into a state of grace, where earthly concerns fade and divine truth illuminates the path ahead.

Furthermore, the use of the Rosary in community settings fosters a profound sense of unity among believers. The act of praying together with shared intentions enhances the communal aspect of faith, transforming individual prayers into a collective plea that reverberates through the heavens. This shared devotion mirrors the early Christian communities, drawing strength and inspiration from collective worship.

In Medjugorje, the Rosary is not just spoken but lived. Pilgrims find themselves swept up in its rhythm, joining hands and hearts with those around them, forming a system of prayers that bind them together in a shared spiritual quest. Each bead becomes a point of connection, a tangible testament to the power of prayer to transcend boundaries and unite souls in the light of divine love.

The role of the Rosary as depicted in the Medjugorje messages also underscores its capacity to bring about peace—both inner and global. The repetition of the "Hail Mary" becomes a mantra, soothing troubled minds and inviting the serenity of God into the chaos of human life. It is a spiritual practice that fosters patience, fortitude, and clarity, qualities essential for navigating the complexities of contemporary existence.

Moreover, the Rosary serves as a powerful catalyst for conversion, inviting believers to examine their lives through the lens of Christ's passion and resurrection. As one contemplates the mysteries of the Rosary, the transformative power of God's love beckons, calling for a renewal of heart and a commitment to living a life steeped in faith. The presence of the Blessed Virgin Mary as a guide further enhances this experience, offering motherly warmth and intercession.

In contemplating the Rosary's role in the messages of Medjugorje, one cannot ignore its capacity to inspire acts of charity and mercy. The Rosary instills a sense of duty to emulate Christ's love for humanity, propelling believers toward actions that reflect His compassion and kindness. It is through the gentle urging of the Rosary that many have found the courage to extend their hands in service to others, becoming vessels of God's love in the world.

Indeed, the Rosary's significance in Medjugorje is deeply tied to a larger vision of peace, hope, and divine intimacy. It is a universal call to prayer, inviting people from all walks of life to embrace the mysteries of faith and to experience the transformative power of God's grace. As the prayers and mysteries of the Rosary weave through the messages of Medjugorje, they invite all to partake in the beauty of divine mystery.

Thus, in the spiritual landscape of Medjugorje, the Rosary stands as a testament to the timeless interplay between Heaven and Earth. It is an instrument of grace that, when embraced with an open heart, illumines the path to profound spiritual awakening and communion with the divine.

Chapter 8: Messages of Fasting

The call to fasting in the messages of Medjugorje reverberates through the corridors of the soul, unraveling the divine will that unites spirit with sacrifice. As the faithful embrace this ancient practice, fasting becomes a profound means of purification, stripping away the ornaments of the mundane world to reveal the divine whisperings within. Paralleling the meditative journey of a desert ascetic, it calls on the devout to offer their hunger as an offering of love, a tangible echo of Christ's own sacrifices. In the rhythmic cadence of abstinence, believers find themselves woven into a celestial narrative, where self-denial melds with grace, and transformative illumination awaits. Through fasting, the faithful do not merely submit to an age-old tradition but step into a divine relationship, embodying the sacred lessons that have echoed from the halls of heaven to the humble village of Medjugorje, aligning their spiritual rhythm with the heartbeat of Sacred Scripture and Tradition.

The Spiritual Benefits of Fasting

In the quiet, unfolding moments of fasting, the mind turns away from the clamor of the world, allowing the soul to be clothed in peaceful clarity. Through centuries, fasting has stood as a profound physical act that breathes life into spiritual ascension. It's not just a renunciation of food; it's a herald of purification, pulling us closer to divine grace. For the faithful making sense of Medjugorje's messages, fasting serves as an unadorned yet mighty bridge connecting human frailty to celestial wisdom.

Just as the people of ancient times sought the divine's favor through fasts, Catholics today mirror this sacred tradition in light of the messages emerging from Medjugorje. These messages are profound whispers from heaven, urging believers to renew their spiritual vigors. Fasting, a recurring theme in these divine communications, provides an escape from earthly bindings, allowing the spirit to ascend and the heart to listen closely to God's gentle whispers.

Through fasting, believers are invited to empty themselves of worldly concerns and invite divine sustenance. In a world layered with distraction and indulgence, this voluntary humility transforms into a gift, allowing Catholics and spiritual seekers alike to refocus on what's unchanging and eternal. It is an activity that goes hand-in-hand with the pursuit of peace—a significant trait found in the messages of Medjugorje.

Fasting is intertwined with prayer, enhancing the efficacy of both. The Old Testament recounts how prophets fasted to speak to God; similarly, these acts of sacrifice align with the invitations from the Blessed Virgin at Medjugorje to deepen prayer life. A fasted body focuses the mind, and a focused mind lends itself to greater participation in prayer, aligning with Mary's call to transform hearts and illuminate souls through fervent devotion.

As in the days when Jesus wandered the wilderness, defeating temptation through fasting, we too find strength in moments of deprivation. The Medjugorje messages recognize fasting not only as personal purification but encourage it as an act of offering for others—those carrying heavier spiritual burdens or navigating life's desolate valleys. This altruism extends fasting's impact, turning what seems a personal act into communal elevation when intentions are set for others' redemption and peace.

The beauty of fasting lies in its simplicity. While the world recognizes bombastic displays of devotion, fasting remains a quieter pursuit. This subtlety does not dilute its power. Rather, it amplifies spirituality, encouraging personal transformation. The Medjugorje messages illuminate pathways to peace, always with fasting as a guidepost, enriching lives through simplicity and discipline.

Fasting also tunes the spirit to discernment, which is particularly substantial in the context of such revelations as given at Medjugorje. A tempered heart is a trainer of virtues. The act becomes a form of spiritual warfare, equipping believers with the virtues of temperance and fortitude, aligning humanity's desires with divine will. Such alignment transforms sinners into saints, as the mothers and fathers of our faith attest.

Furthermore, fasting can be seen as an offering, a sacrificial act of surrender to God's will—similar to the ultimate sacrifice of the Cross. Through fasting, the faithful echo Christ's own desert trial and triumph over fleshly desires, entering into a communion of suffering that births understanding and empathy. This sacred act deepens the spiritual journey, enriching the spirit as it resonates with the messages of intercession and peace found in Medjugorje.

While fasting primarily signifies spiritual purpose, it can't be ignored that it holds potential health benefits. A fasted body often reflects in clearer thoughts and purified intentions. Yet, true spiritual fasting transcends tangible gain—it becomes about discovering strength in spiritual poverty. By embracing hunger for spiritual fulfillment, believers unlock doors to a deeper, transformative relationship with the divine.

Exercising the practice of fasting, devotees contribute to global spiritual well-being, mirroring a unity that transcends cultural divides. In Medjugorje, fasting becomes a shared spiritual vocabulary, as unique as a fingerprint yet connecting the faithful through prayer and sacrifice—a language that transcends words to articulate an aspiration towards divine union.

In summary, the spiritual benefits of fasting as illustrated through Medjugorje's revelations are manifold. It is this dual purpose, both personal and communal, which heartens and fortifies individuals on their journey towards God. By turning away from excess and embracing simplicity, believers engage in a transformative act that resonates with the divine blueprint etched into the messages of Medjugorje. As this celestial dialog continues to unfold, fasting remains an unwavering bastion of faith, challenging believers to transcend beyond earthly confines and seek a soul-awakening kinship with the divine.

Integrating Fasting into Daily Life

Fasting, often perceived as a relic of ancient practice, emerges as a guiding light in the messages from Medjugorje. Traditionally observed during Lent, fasting is more than mere deprivation; it's a profound spiritual tool that aligns with heaven's call to deepen our connection with God. Within the messages conveyed by Our Lady, fasting is not just an act but a lifestyle, a recurring theme echoing through the corridors of biblical history.

The ancient scriptural roots of fasting remind us of its purpose: a means to purification, an ascent toward holiness, and a weapon against the subtlety of sin. In a world overflowing with abundance, the Medjugorje messages challenge the faithful to confront the pervasive allure of materialism by integrating fasting into daily life. While some may balk at the idea, viewing it as archaic or extreme, the allure of fasting lies not in its challenge but in its transformative power.

The practice of fasting invites the practitioner into a space of dependency and relinquishment. It offers an opportunity to detach from worldly pleasures and refocus on the divine, aligning one's desires with God's will. By integrating fasting into daily routines, as suggested by the Medjugorje messages, the faithful are encouraged to transform mundane acts of abstention into vibrant expressions of faith.

The alluring allegory of the desert—a place of temptation boldly confronted by Christ himself—resonates within the practice of fasting. It serves as a retreat from worldly distractions, guiding the soul into a profound dialogue with the Almighty. It is here, in this sacred space, that the faithful are urged to listen intently, to seek guidance, and to emerge strengthened. As we deny ourselves the comforts of daily consumption, we create a vacuum for grace to fill, amplifying the divine within us.

In adopting a lifestyle of fasting, one finds parallels with the saints who walked the path of piety. Numerous saints have extolled fasting as an integral practice for spiritual life, demonstrating that it is more than a superficial denial. In their wisdom, fasting refines the soul, heightening virtues of patience, humility, and charity. Our Lady's messages underscore this saintly tradition, reinforcing that through fasting, one's spiritual senses are sharpened, alert to the whispers of divine providence.

An alluring epic unfolds when fasting transcends mere ritual. For those in search of holiness, fasting is akin to a sacred journey. It becomes an exodus from the bonds of self-indulgence, a pilgrimage not to the physical lands of Medjugorje but to an internal landscape where heaven meets the human heart. In this ongoing journey, the call to fast becomes an anthem of solidarity with Christ's own desert sojourn.

Those adopting fasting as a devotional practice may start gradually, incorporating it in simple yet meaningful ways. The commitment can begin with minor sacrifices, such as skipping a meal, refraining from a favorite indulgence, or substituting meal times with prayer or reflection. These modest steps, grounded in the Medjugorje messages, build discipline and foster spiritual growth, realigning the heart's focus on eternal truths.

As the faithful immerse themselves in fasting, community plays a pivotal role. Drawing from the communal practices revered in monastic traditions, shared fasting experiences can galvanize believers, intertwining their individual efforts into a collective testament of faith. In Medjugorje's communal setting, fasting nurtures unity, reminding the faithful that they are part of a larger, divine narrative.

Furthermore, the practice aligns with biblical teachings and the core of Catholic spirituality. When embraced collectively within families or parishes, fasting enriches spiritual bonds, fostering a communal spirit of sacrifice and prayer. It becomes a rallying cry for spiritual vigilance, cultivating an environment ripe for the seeds of divine conversion and blessings to flourish.

The call to fasting articulated in Medjugorje messages draws inspiration from echoes of biblical lamentation and triumph. It's a call to renew and transform; fasting thus becomes a channel for grace, intercession, and a profound act of love towards God and neighbor alike. It inspires the believer to live in the sacred rhythm of fasting and feasting, echoing the divine dance between discipline and celebration.

With every fast, the faithful respond to a heavenly invitation to sanctity, to participate intimately in the mystery of Christ's passion. Within this narrative, fasting is much more than a practice; it is a call, a vocation toward holiness that reorients the soul to its source of eternal joy. By listening to the Medjugorje messages, embracing fasting in daily life is seen not as an imposition but as a divine enrichment, fostering joy and spiritual renewal.

In essence, the messages of Medjugorje resonate with an ancient yet timeless call: to seek God above all things. As fasting becomes ingrained in daily life, it transcends its traditional confines, revealing its role as a contemporary fixture of faith and devotion. The interaction between earthly restraint and divine largesse reflects a harmonious symphony composed by the divine conductor.

However, advocating for a fasting lifestyle also necessitates wisdom and compassion. The practices must adapt to individual health needs and abilities, allowing every believer to partake in the spiritual fruits of fasting without jeopardizing physical well-being. This echoes the compassionate guidance found in Our Lady's messages, prompting each soul to discern its path in unity with God's will.

By drawing these practices together, the devotional act of fasting, as guided by the Medjugorje messages, emerges as an integral part of a devout life. Fasting, when integrated holistically, fortifies the soul, readies the heart, and channels divine grace into the marrow of one's existence. It fulfills its sacred purpose in drawing us closer to the heart of Christ, nurturing a life centered on heavenly truths that transcend the ephemeral shadows of the world.

Chapter 9: Messages of Faith

In the quiet brilliance of Medjugorje's sunlit skies, the messages of faith come alive with divine whispers that kindle the spirit, sparking revelations that transcend the earthly realm. Each message, a beacon of celestial light, invites the faithful to immerse themselves in a deeper relationship with the Holy Trinity, fostering trust and unwavering devotion. As the seers recount their encounters, the intertwining of Heaven's truth with human frailty becomes manifest, calling believers to anchor their lives in the promises bestowed from above. Echoing through the valleys and hearts is an exhortation to embrace faith as a living, dynamic force—one that empowers not just endurance in trials but a transformation into vessels of grace and carriers of divine love. Through these sacred exchanges, a tapestry unfolds, intricately woven with threads of belief and trust, each thread shimmering with the essence of the holy messages delivered. These revelations are not mere words but an invitation to embody the virtues espoused by Christ, nurturing seeds of faith that blossom into acts of compassion and forgiveness, resonating with the timeless teachings of Sacred Scripture and Tradition.

Strengthening Faith Through the Messages

The enigmatic village of Medjugorje, nestled between the rugged hills of Bosnia and Herzegovina, stands as a beacon for those seeking spiritual renewal. The messages emanating from this sacred place are more than whispered prayers carried by the wind; they are a profound testament to the potential of faith reinforced by celestial guidance. Faith is not a static commodity, but an evolving journey, and the revelations in Medjugorje invite believers to embark on this transformative journey with renewed vigor.

The messages delivered through the seers of Medjugorje are remarkable in their simplicity and depth, serving as a gentle yet insistent call to a deeper spiritual life. One must ask: what does it mean for faith to be strengthened? It's a question as old as Christianity itself, woven into the fabric of biblical legend and theological inquiry. Strength isn't merely the fortitude to face adversity; it is also the capacity to embrace the uncertainties of the divine with unwavering trust. These messages reach into the depths of the spirit, echoing the calls of ancient prophets while simultaneously stirring the soul's modern yearning.

In their essence, the messages of Medjugorje emphasize the elements central to any profound Christian faith: love, charity, sacrifice, and prayer. They call on the world not merely to listen but to act, transforming lives through simple yet profoundly significant decisions—the kind that align with the teachings of Christ. Through daily adherence to these messages, an individual's faith becomes a living response to divine will, manifesting in acts seen and unseen.

Consider the allegory of a tree planted by the rivers of water, an image well familiar from the Psalms. Just as the tree's roots draw sustenance from the river, so too does a person's faith draw its strength from the living waters of Medjugorje's revelations. These messages encourage believers to examine their faith's roots, nurturing them with prayer and sacrifice, ensuring that they are firmly planted in the rich soil of tradition and Scripture.

Efficiently, the messages serve as both a mirror and a compass, reflecting one's spiritual state while pointing toward a transcendent path. They remind believers of the power inherent in shared faith; a communal strength binds individuals together, buoying them through trials and triumphs alike. In Medjugorje, the shared experience of receiving these messages creates a palpable sense of interconnected faith that amplifies personal convictions.

One particularly moving aspect of the Medjugorje messages is their consistency with Sacred Tradition and Sacred Scripture. Such consistency offers reassurance that, while the world around us—replete with distractions and doubts—may change, the core truths of faith remain steadfast. This alignment not only underscores the authenticity of the messages but also imbues them with an authority that compels believers to take heed and incorporate them into their daily lives.

For biblical scholars, the harmonization of these messages with traditional Church teachings provides fertile ground for reflection and analysis. It prompts a reevaluation of how ancient texts resonate through contemporary revelations, offering a reminder of God's unchanging nature and His constant presence in the lives of the faithful.

Spiritualists, on the other hand, might focus on the meditative quality of the messages. Drawing from the profound silence of meditation, each message is a call towards personal introspection and transcendence. It is a journey inward that reveals the divine mystery through contemplative practice, nurturing a personal encounter with the divine.

One cannot ignore the testimonies that emerge from those whose lives have radically changed after embracing the Medjugorje messages. These stories, while unique in their particulars, share a common thread: individuals report an overwhelming sense of peace, clarity, and purpose after engaging with the messages. Their renewed faith is often characterized by an increased zeal for prayer, a commitment to charity, and a profound sense of connection to the Church's communal body.

The epic narrative of faith finds fresh articulation as these messages, both new and ancient, call to souls weary from life's battles. The spiritual serenity and strength that many report after tapping into this divine wellspring are testaments to the messages' efficacy and transformative potential. Such stories warm even the most skeptical heart, serving not just as anecdotes but as living testimonies of faith's complexity and beauty.

While messages themselves are pivotal, it is the conversion they inspire that stands as the true hallmark of their power. Conversion isn't merely about changing beliefs but involves a metamorphosis of the heart and soul—becoming a new creation infused with divine love and purpose. Each step along this transformative journey rooted in Medjugorje's insights culminates in a faith not only fortified but imbued with renewed vitality.

In examining how faith is strengthened through these heavenly messages, one must not overlook the role of community and shared experience. Pilgrimages to Medjugorje create spaces where individuals not only encounter the divine but also share this sacred experience with others, fostering a collective spiritual resilience that supports individual growth. This shared pilgrimage of faith, both literal and metaphorical, amplifies the messages' impact, turning personal revelation into widespread spiritual renewal.

Thus, returning to the core question of what it means to have one's faith strengthened, we find our answer in the actions and transformations that follow the receiving of these messages. Faith is an ongoing narrative, a living dialogue with the divine, and the Medjugorje messages provide chapters of profound insight and inspiration within that dialogue.

Therefore, as the messages of Medjugorje continue their journey across the world, their call resonates ever deeper. They hold the potential to reshape hearts, deepen connections, and forge unbreakable bonds of faith—a testament, indeed, to divine providence and love.

These insights encourage us to listen, to act, and ultimately, to allow our faith to flourish in ways we might never have imagined.

Testimonies of Deepened Faith

In the embrace of Medjugorje's serenity, countless souls have found their faith strengthened, as if an invisible thread from heaven gently wove itself into the fabric of their spiritual lives. Pilgrims, in sharing their encounters, often return transformed, their hearts carrying the indelible mark of deeper conviction. The messages brought forth from the apparitions have acted as a key, unlocking a profound sense of belief and commitment in the faithful.

Consider the testimony of a man who, burdened with doubts and uncertainties, found solace under the starry cloak of Medjugorje's night sky. He recounts how a quiet whisper in his heart, prompted by a message of surrender and trust in Divine Providence, unraveled the knots of skepticism. The encounter transformed his hesitant steps into a resolute path of unwavering faith. His story, like many others, underscores the unfolding mystery that the messages from Medjugorje are not just words but divine instruments that perform spiritual alchemy in human hearts.

For a mother overwhelmed by the demands of life, the invitation to live a life of prayer, fasting, and peace in Medjugorje rekindled a flame that nearly flickered out. Her firsthand experience of the profound hush in the chapel, amidst a community of believers, ignited a vibrant faith. She realized that this pilgrimage had penetrated her soul, unveiling a clarity that came not from her understanding, but from a divine gift received in Medjugorje. Her newfound devotion bore fruit back home as she embraced the Marian call to pray the Rosary daily, breathing life into her routine with grace and intention.

The poignant day when a skeptical academic stood in the sacred fields of Medjugorje, she didn't expect her heart to soften. However, drawn by an unexplainable allure, she opened herself to a transcendent reality she'd never dared to accept. Her logical mind, well-acquainted with theological doctrines, met the humble simplicity and profound honesty of Medjugorje's messages. This encounter shattered her intellectual defenses, nurturing a deeper, more earnest faith that blended the rigor of her scholarship with the humility of a childlike trust.

These stories form a construct of testimonies revealing how Medjugorje acts as a catalyst for spiritual renewal. Pilgrims find themselves swept into a whirlwind of divine love through messages that resonate with ancient Scriptural wisdom and modern relevance. A young seminarian, once disheartened and on the brink of abandoning his vocation, spoke of a message that highlighted perseverance and the quiet power of the Holy Spirit. This illumination reinvigorated his pursuit of priesthood, instilling in him a newfound vigor he attributes to the reassuring messages from Our Lady.

As layers of disbelief peel away, many find a deep and abiding faith anchored in the heart's core. The testimony of a businessman, who came seeking answers to questions he didn't even know he had, speaks volumes of Medjugorje's influence. Amidst his hectic life, the messages instilled a reminder that his spirituality could guide rather than compete with his ambitions. It was here, he claims, that he rediscovered the ancient art of balancing his earthly pursuits with the spiritual gifts he had long ignored.

Medjugorje, with its ethereal messages, serves as a spiritual forge where faith is not just professed but lived and deeply felt. A dialogue emerges between heaven and earth, where the soul learns to dance to the rhythms of hope, peace, and love. A single message can spark a transformative journey—where merely believing morphs into an intimate, living experience of faith. For the elderly couple, each step they take is a testament to how Medjugorje's messages urged them to rediscover their first love, God, and in doing so, renewed their commitment to each other.

The testimonies are bound together by personal transformation and a collective faith journey. A medical doctor, whose life revolved around empirical evidence, found his heart opening to miraculous possibilities after a visit to Medjugorje. Witnessing the unexplainable recovery of a fellow pilgrim, he embraced the mystery of divine intervention with humility, allowing his faith to transcend scientific boundaries. His experience epitomized a moment where faith met reason, where divine mystery wrapped its arms around human understanding.

Such stories echo with a profound realization that Medjugorje, with its messages, is a gentle requiem that awakens the sleeping spirit. It invites everyone on a journey—an invitation not to see, but to believe, to embrace the unknown with trust, and experience an unforeseen deepening of faith. Herein, the seers' revelations animate believers, infusing life into ancient prophecy, and turning theological concepts into heart-lived truths. The intangible becomes tangible, and the unseen is vividly felt.

As these testimonies resound through time, they affirm Medjugorje as a sacred place where heaven's words meticulously integrate into daily life. It's a place where the believer, journeying through the valleys of doubt and over the peaks of insight, discovers that the messages are indeed a divine compass guiding them back to their eternal home. For many, faith that began as a flickering candle is kindled into a blazing beacon by the miraculous encounters and messages experienced there. The shared stories form a sacred symphony, an exquisite expression of faith that transcends the ordinary, drawing all closer to the divine love ever present in human lives.

Chapter 10: Messages of Conversion

In the quiet moments of introspection, amidst the mystical hills of Medjugorje, the call to conversion echoes with a resounding urgency that pierces the soul. The seers speak of transformation not as a distant ideal, but as an imminent reality that beckons each one of us towards a profound metamorphosis. Conversion here is less about a single moment of enlightenment and more a continuous journey guided by Our Lady's gentle admonitions. As we traverse this spiritual path, we are drawn into a dynamic dance with the divine, where grace and free will intertwine, sparking a renewal akin to the wayward Saul on the road to Damascus. The testimonies of conversion from those who have heeded this celestial call illuminate the narrative with awe-inspiring tales of hearts turned from stone to flesh, of lives reconfigured from chaos to peace. Through these messages, we are urged to abandon our complacency, to confront the shadows within, and to embrace the vibrant gift of faith that Medjugorje offers. Here, conversion is not an end, but the very heartbeat of a spiritual renaissance, weaving us into a living testament of God's unyielding love and mercy.

Understanding Conversion in Medjugorje

In the heart of Medjugorje, where visions have captivated the hearts and minds of countless pilgrims, lies the profound call to conversion. Conversion, a transforming embrace of faith that reshapes lives, pulses as a central theme in the messages bestowed upon the seers. This metamorphosis is not merely a change in religious affiliation or the simple acceptance of certain doctrines. Instead, it is a profound internal transformation—a rebirth of the spirit that aligns one's life with the divine will as epitomized in the messages of Medjugorje.

The essence of these conversion messages draws deeply from a wellspring of hope. At its core, conversion in Medjugorje is viewed as a journey, a pilgrimage of the soul that mirrors the physical pilgrimage many undertake to this sacred place. Just as a pilgrim's journey is marked by steps and stages, so too is the inward journey of conversion. It involves a conscious and deliberate turning away from sin and a sincere turning towards God, an act reminiscent of St. Augustine's own conversion, which he so beautifully discusses in his "Confessions." A yearning for renewal, akin to Augustine's restless heart finding rest in God, echoes through the messages given in Medjugorje.

This call to conversion is enveloped in profound simplicity. The messages implore individuals to return to fundamental spiritual practices, to embrace the sacraments, and to rediscover the peace found in prayer and reflection. Through these practices, believers are gently guided back to the essence of their faith, rediscovering the gentle whispers of divine love that lead to a fuller, more robust relationship with God. In a world often filled with noise, Medjugorje's messages beckon the faithful to quietude, where the soul can hear the soft calling of conversion that echoes the tranquility of moments spent in intimate prayer.

An intriguing aspect of conversion in Medjugorje is its communal dimension. While deeply personal, conversion also involves the broader community of believers. The transformation of individuals in Medjugorje reverberates through families, parishes, and communities, creating a ripple effect that extends beyond individual boundaries. This communal transformation can be likened to the biblical account of Pentecost, where the Holy Spirit's descent ignites a flame within individuals that spreads through collective action and inspiration. The messages thus invite not just personal conversion, but also a reawakening of communal faith and action.

A striking feature of Medjugorje's conversion messages is their alignment with Sacred Scripture and Sacred Tradition. The messages echo Christ's call to repentance found in the Gospels, seamlessly weaving scriptural truths with contemporary exhortations to live out the Gospel in everyday life. This continuity with Sacred Tradition serves as both a reassurance and a challenge to believers, urging them to embody the faith in a manner consistent with the Church's timeless teachings. There lies a certain poetic beauty in this synthesis, a dance between the ancient and the contemporary that breathes new life into the timeless call to conversion.

Conversion in Medjugorje is not an abstract ideal but a practical, lived experience. It is exemplified in the testimonies of countless pilgrims who have walked Medjugorje's stony paths, entering with hearts burdened by sin and doubt, and leaving renewed, filled with a sense of peace and purpose. These personal transformations stand as living testaments to the power and reality of conversion in this Marian shrine. The personal stories of conversion bear witness to a profound grace that transcends human understanding, inviting others to embark on their own journeys of transformation.

Furthermore, the messages of conversion in Medjugorje emphasize the enduring hope of the human spirit's capacity for change. Conversion is not a one-time event but an ongoing process, a journey that invites continual growth and deeper understanding of God's love. This dynamic process mirrors the Church's teaching on conversion as lifelong, a continuous turning toward God even after lapses or failures. Through Medjugorje, this message of ongoing conversion offers hope and encouragement, underscoring that no soul is beyond the reach of divine mercy and transformation.

Ultimately, understanding conversion in Medjugorje invites introspection and a re-examination of personal faith journeys. It challenges individuals to delve deeper into their own spiritual lives, to seek out areas in need of conversion, and to respond to the divine invitation to renewal. The messages extend a gentle yet compelling call, urging each believer to embark on this transformative journey with courage and faith. In embracing this call, one steps into a narrative that is as ancient as it is new, a story of redemption and hope that binds together the faithful in a collective journey toward spiritual renewal.

Personal Testimonies of Conversion

The story of Medjugorje is not just a tale of visions and messages; it's a profound narrative of transformation, resonating deeply in the lives of many who have encountered it. The journey of conversion, often a pivotal moment in a pilgrim's life, is sometimes quiet and subtle, other times intense and immediate. Yet, for countless individuals, it marks the beginning of a new spiritual chapter. In these testimonies, one finds the essence of grace that flows unceasingly from this sacred place.

Consider the account of John, a man whose life was shadowed by skepticism. A successful entrepreneur, John prided himself on rationality and practicality, often dismissing spiritual matters as folklore. Persuaded by a close friend to visit Medjugorje, he approached the pilgrimage with a courteous cynicism. However, the peace that enveloped him on the first evening drew him in, almost against his will. As he listened to the seers and absorbed the atmosphere of devotion, a quiet transformation began. By the end of his visit, John found himself contemplating the rosary, a symbol he had previously regarded as merely ornamental. In those beads, he discovered a path to reflection and prayer that reoriented his life's purpose.

In a similarly moving narrative, we encounter Maria, a woman burdened with grief. Her daughter, a victim of a tragic accident, left Maria deeply wounded, questioning her faith and the existence of a loving God. Her journey to Medjugorje was a desperate search for consolation. During her time there, Maria experienced a sense of release, an unexplainable peace that she hadn't known since before her tragedy. In the confessional, a profound conversation with a priest became the turning point. She described the moment as if a great weight was lifted from her heart, allowing her to feel her daughter's presence, now in a place of joyful light. This newfound peace didn't erase her loss but offered her a framework to live on with hope and acceptance.

Stories like these abound, each as unique as the souls who tell them. Emma, a young college student struggling with identity and belonging, found in Medjugorje the acceptance and love she yearned for. Her conversion was not marked by thunderous revelations but by a gentle realization of self-love and divine love. Watching the crowds kneeling in prayer and experiencing the communal joy of worship, Emma discovered a kinship with the faithful, understanding for the first time her place within the order of creation. For her, these were the threads that wove her back to faith.

Then there's Carlos, whose testimony highlights the awakening of spiritual senses long dormant. Raised in a secular environment, he embarked on this pilgrimage out of curiosity, spurred by tales of miracles. Initially bemused by the devotion he observed, he gradually became aware of an inner stirring. One evening, transfixed by the setting sun against the Cross Mountain, Carlos found his heart open to something beyond logic. His conversion was marked by a profound silence, a moment he describes as having the veil of the mundane lifted, revealing a universe alive with meaning and divine presence. From that experience, he returned to his life with a renewed perspective, seeing God's fingerprints in every detail of existence.

Matthew's walk towards conversion involved confronting personal demons. Plagued by addiction, he journeyed to Medjugorje at a friend's insistence, more to placate than to find redemption. Yet, the spiritual ambiance of the town began to seep into his bones. Struggling with withdrawal, he spent nights in restless prayer, wrestling with physical and spiritual chains. It was within the gentle embrace of Medjugorje's serenity that Matthew glimpsed the possibility of freedom. He left with resolve, bolstered by a newfound community and faith that sustains him daily, a living testament to the healing power of faith encounters.

The convert's path, while uniquely tailored to individual journeys, consistently echoes with themes of healing, hope, and renewal. Each testimony, as varied as the myriad languages spoken by pilgrims, adds to the complex mosaic of Medjugorje's influence. Through these personal narratives, the world witnesses the radiant evidence of Medjugorje's heavenly origin, where ordinary lives intersect with divine love, confirming that these experiences, these conversions, are not merely figments of pious imaginations but tangible realities aligning with the sacred traditions of faith and scripture.

Faithful testimonies speak volumes to the power and divine orchestration that underlies the messages of Medjugorje. They serve as beacons, illuminating the way for others who seek transformation. Indeed, in reflecting on these stories, one perceives a grasp of the mysterious yet intimate ways God can touch hearts, crafting stories of redemption and love that not only mirror biblical accounts but expand them into the ongoing narrative of salvation.

Medjugorje's role as a catalyst for conversion inspires both those firmly rooted in their faith and those adrift. Whether through the whispers of Mary's messages, shared in quiet moments of prayer or through the companionship of fellow pilgrims, it becomes apparent that Medjugorje is a conduit through which God's grace flows abundantly, inviting perpetual conversion of heart.

Chapter 11: Aligning with Sacred Tradition

In the sacred history of the Catholic faith, tradition and revelation are threads woven together with divine precision, guiding the faithful through the ages. The messages of Medjugorje, with their ethereal echo, find their place alongside the eternal wisdom of Sacred Tradition. As the apparitions unfurl their messages, they offer a divine consonance that harmonizes with the profound truths revered by the Church. Here, the celestial whispers not only align with the canonical scriptures but also resonate deeply with the hearts nurtured by centuries of devout practice. These messages stand not as isolated phenomena but as part of a perennial conversation between heaven and earth, enriching the spiritual journey with an invitation to rediscover ancient truths through a contemporary lens. In embracing these divine communiqués, believers are called to a profound synthesis, one that respects the continuum of tradition while opening to the fervent winds of spiritual renewal and assurance from the heart of Medjugorje.

The Role of Tradition in Medjugorje Messages

In understanding the messages from Medjugorje, it's crucial to appreciate how deeply they are intertwined with Sacred Tradition. Tradition carries within it the voice of the Apostles, echoed through the ages, a whispered yet unwavering truth that both informs and validates private revelations. The Medjugorje messages do not stand as isolated whispers of the divine but as vibrant affirmations of the Christian continuity that began some two millennia ago.

Sacred Tradition serves as a guiding compass, steering the faithful and the inquiring soul toward the heart of divine truth. In the messages received by the seers in Medjugorje, there's a repository of ancient wisdom constructed anew, resonating with the teachings and practices preserved in the Church's sacred deposit of faith. They echo the call to holiness, repentance, and unwavering trust in God's plan—an echo that aligns with the ageless cadence of traditional Church teachings.

Embedded in the messages of Medjugorje is a call to return to the roots of the faith—to prayer, fasting, and the sacraments. These are pillars that the Church has long held as essential to fostering a vibrant spiritual life. The messages, while new in their delivery, are old in their essence, reminding believers to nourish their souls through timeless practices. This aligning with Sacred Tradition reinforces their authenticity and invites believers to engage deeply with the spiritual gifts offered by the Church.

The rich history of Sacred Tradition is not merely a passive backdrop but a dynamic and living reality that gives shape to the messages proclaimed by Our Lady of Medjugorje. In urging endless prayer and repentance, the messages reinforce that flow of grace which has been part of the continuous, unbroken tradition from the Apostolic Fathers to today's believers. This alignment suggests a divine orchestration, where past, present, and future converge within the cradle of the Church's sacred legacy.

Moreover, the messages of Medjugorje illuminate the intricate relationship between Tradition and personal spiritual growth. The messages advocate a profound introspection, a commitment to inner transformation that has resonated with Catholics through the ages. This call to personal holiness, so inherent in the messages, is a cornerstone of Tradition, offering believers a way to live authentically in communion with the divine.

In a world that often wavers under the weight of skepticism and soft whispers of doubt, the embrace of Tradition in the messages provides a foundation of firm conviction. From the insistence on the sacraments to the practice of virtues, these messages revive what has been taught, lived, and cherished within the Church since its earliest days. They remind us that the foundation of faith is as relevant today as it was centuries ago.

One cannot ignore the seamless weaving of the Rosary's significance—a practice deeply rooted in Tradition—within the calls from Medjugorje. Our Lady's encouragement for daily recitation ties believers to a historical devotion that has served as a spiritual weapon, comfort, and guide for countless Christians. This demonstrates that the Medjugorje messages reaffirm and reignite the love for these time-honored practices, enveloping the faithful in a cocoon of divine reassurance.

Indeed, the alignment with Tradition in the messages serves not merely as a repetition of the past but as a renewal. It is an invitation to see the living Tradition not as a relic, but as a vibrant and active conveyor of grace. The messages urge the modern Catholic to bridge the historical with the contemporary, to recognize Tradition as a living, breathing testimony that speaks to every soul willing to listen.

The Medjugorje messages also touch on ethical and moral directions that thread through the heart of Catholic teaching. They call on individuals to uphold their baptismal promises, encouraging them to embody Christian virtues. This moral compass, long maintained by Tradition, finds a new voice in the directives from Medjugorje, reminding believers of their divine heritage and responsibilities.

Additionally, the messages propel the faithful to delve deeper into the mystery of the Eucharist—another pillar of Sacred Tradition. This exploration is a journey back to the Last Supper, an invitation to the mystical union that transcends time and space. Thus, Medjugorje seamlessly connects the everyday with the eternal, offering a vivid testament to Tradition's timeless relevance.

The Medjugorje messages carry with them the potency of Tradition, serving both as a torch lighting the path and a compass guiding the pilgrim. Through these messages, the ancient and the new come together in a divine dance, harmonizing with the eternal symphony of the Church's sacred Tradition. As such, they stand as both a call and a challenge to awaken, to engage, and to live out the timeless truths that have been revealed and cherished for centuries. In embracing these messages, believers are invited not only to listen but to weave themselves into the living fabric of Tradition, ensuring its vitality for generations to come.

Examining Tradition and Scripture

In the heart of Roman Catholicism lies a profound reverence for Sacred Tradition and Sacred Scripture, the dual pillars upon which faith is built. The apparitions at Medjugorje have sparked a quest among the faithful to discern how these celestial messages align with the foundational beliefs handed down through generations. As we delve into this examination, it is essential to consider the essence of both Tradition and Scripture, and how they converge in the context of Medjugorje.

Tradition, in its most ancient sense, represents the living transmission of the faith. It is not merely a set of customs or practices, but rather a vibrant thread linking the faithful across time and space. The messages from Medjugorje often echo themes deeply rooted in this Tradition. For instance, their emphasis on prayer, repentance, and conversion resonate with the age-old call of the Church to holiness. Such elements have perpetually been present since the early Church Fathers, manifesting the continuity of divine calls through history.

In contrast, Scripture is the written testament of God's word, a profound source of spiritual nourishment and guidance. The seers' messages, while contemporary, are steeped in biblical allegory and symbology. Drawing parallels to biblical narratives, the apparitions and messages reflect themes of peace and salvation reminiscent of the proclamations found in both the Old and New Testaments. The visionaries' experiences and the messages they convey often mirror the prophetic calls to return to God's grace seen throughout biblical history.

The Old Testament, with its tales of prophets and divine interventions, offers a rich canon against which the Medjugorje experiences can be measured. Consider the recurring call to repentance, akin to the prophetic urgings of Isaiah or Jeremiah. Such a summons is not confined to antiquity but resounds through the corridors of Catholic spirituality, where Medjugorje continues this sacred call. There is a profound alignment here—a continuity of divine instruction urging humanity towards transformation and reconciliation with the Creator.

The New Testament further fortifies this alignment, especially within the Gospels and the epistles of the Apostles. The Medjugorje messages often accentuate Christ's call to love, echoing the honesty of the Beatitudes. The invitation to embody the virtues spoken on the Sermon on the Mount encapsulates the essence of Christian living, which is so dear to the Sacred Tradition. Inherently, these messages encourage believers to live the Gospel with sincerity, highlighting the congruence of the supernatural with Christ's teachings.

Moreover, the messages of Medjugorje, much like the parables of Christ, are often rich in symbolism and allegory. They invite a deep contemplative response, urging the faithful to discern beyond literal meanings. Such a method reflects the allegorical style of biblical teachings, where hidden truths are unearthed through meditation and spiritual insight. The sacred tradition of lectio divina, an ancient practice of prayerful reading of Scripture, finds a natural companion in reflecting on these heavenly messages, both demanding an engaged and contemplative heart.

Aligned with this, the Catechism of the Catholic Church offers insight into how private revelations, like those at Medjugorje, should be approached. While not adding to the deposit of faith, these revelations bear the function of guiding and edifying the faithful in practicing the Gospel. Within this framework, the messages from Medjugorje are evaluated critically by the Church to protect the integrity of the faith and ensure that such revelations are harmonious with established beliefs. This discernment process contributes to the Church's commitment to upholding Truth.

In light of Tradition and Scripture, Medjugorje is a living testament to the continuous revelation of God's will. It serves as a reminder that the divine narrative is not static— God's interaction with humanity is dynamic and ongoing. As stewards of faith, Catholics are called to weigh these messages, appreciating the intricate confluence of the past with present expressions of divine initiative. Through prayerful consideration and discernment, the faithful can navigate these revelations, understanding them as a contemporary echo of Gospel truths and ancient Traditions.

This exploration compels one to not only acknowledge the messages themselves but to actively participate in the spirituality they propose. The sacred Tradition encourages the witnessing of faith through action, a principle underscored by the messages that advocate for living faith robustly. By embracing the teachings of Medjugorje, Catholics worldwide are invited into a deeper relationship with Christ, fulfilling Tradition's call to enact God's love in the world.

In conclusion, the examination of Tradition and Scripture in the context of Medjugorje is not a mere academic endeavor but a spiritual journey. It invites believers to engage with their faith dynamically, discerning the interplay between old and new revelations. As Medjugorje continues to touch hearts and ignite faith, it stands as a testament to the enduring power of Sacred Tradition and Sacred Scripture, harmonizing the eternal with the temporal in the sacred journey towards God.

Chapter 12: Practical Instructions from Our Lady

In this chapter, we delve into the cherished guidance that Our Lady imparts, offering a compass for daily spiritual growth that reverberates with timeless wisdom. These instructions, as revealed through the visionaries, are both profound and accessible, encouraging a life imbued with prayerful dedication and heartfelt devotion. Our Lady's message resonates with echoes of simplicity and truth, urging believers to weave these practices into the fabric of everyday existence. By embracing these sacred routines, such as consistent prayer, contemplation, and acts of charity, the faithful cultivate a life that mirrors the Gospel's call to holiness. This divine guidance, tenderly aligned with Sacred Tradition and Scripture, becomes not only a path to personal transformation but a beacon of hope in a world thirsty for spiritual renewal. Our Lady's invitation is a gentle yet compelling summons to realign our lives with divine purpose, reminding us that these holy practices are not relics of the past but living instructions meant to illuminate paths in today's ever-complex world.

Daily Practices for Spiritual Growth

In the quiet moments of life, the bustle fades and there is a chance to look inward, to find spiritual renewal through practices that have been whispered to us by Our Lady in the peaceful village of Medjugorje. These daily practices are not merely routines but doorways to a deeper connection with the Divine, a way to align our lives with heavenly wisdom and the embrace of Sacred Tradition and Sacred Scripture. Practices inspired by Medjugorje offer a rhythmic cadence to our days—a harmony that moves with the tides of joy and sorrow, guiding us toward spiritual maturity.

The Rosary stands as a potent pillar among these practices, a daily prayer that is less about rote recitation and more a heart-felt dialogue with the Divine. In each bead and every Hail Mary, there lies an opportunity to meditate on the mysteries of faith. It's said that through the repetition of prayer, our souls are tuned to the frequency of heaven. This devotion nurtures the soul, an embrace between the believer and the Mother of God that echoes the rituals and meditative practices upheld by countless saints before us.

Equally transformative is the practice of fasting, though often misunderstood in modern parlance. Fasting in the context of spiritual growth transcends the physical act of abstention; it's a disciplined path that clears the clutter of excess from our lives. When aligned with prayer, fasting becomes a powerful tool to purify the spirit, aligning us more closely with the sacrificial heart of Christ. It's not merely about 'giving up' but about receiving an abundance of grace and strength, centering one's intentions on the needs of the soul rather than the demands of the body.

In Medjugorje, Our Lady calls for the reading of Sacred Scripture as another daily practice. The Scriptures are not just historical text; they are living words that breathe life into our existence. This daily engagement opens us to divine wisdom, urging believers to ponder and to act in ways that transform the mundane into the sacred. As one threads through the stories and teachings of the Bible, there is an invitation to find personal meaning and growth in its eternal truths.

Perhaps overlooked but immensely powerful is the daily practice of examining one's conscience. This reflection is not an exercise in judgment but one in grace. By daily considering our actions, attitudes, and thoughts, we allow our spiritual self to shed its imperfections like an autumn tree surrendering its leaves. Such introspection aligns with the age-old teachings of reconciliation and penance, pathways that enable a deeper connection with God's perpetual forgiveness and love.

Alongside these practices, Our Lady emphasizes the profound simplicity and humbling act of performing acts of charity as part of daily spiritual routines. Charity, in its truest sense, is the manifestation of love. It's the outpouring of grace received through prayer and reflection into the world—a way to actualize Christ's compassion and mercy. Whether a simple smile to a stranger or assistance given to those in need, such acts enrich both the giver and the receiver, adding layers of grace to daily life.

Adoration of the Blessed Sacrament also carries significant importance as a transformative daily practice. This quiet, contemplative time in the presence of the Eucharist offers a sacred pause amidst life's chaos. Here, the heart finds solace and strength, the spirit is replenished, and one is enveloped in divine love. It's a moment where the transcendent becomes tangible, allowing God's peace to permeate into the depths of our being.

The daily practice of seeking silence—or intentional times of silence—is another profound way to nurture spiritual growth. In a world dominated by noise and distraction, finding a quiet corner to retreat can be a precious gift. Silence isn't merely the absence of sound but the presence of God. In these serene moments, the soul can listen more intently to the whispers of divine wisdom, fostering a deeper communion with the Sacred.

Forging a daily relationship with Our Lady through personal prayer and meditation invites her guidance and maternal protection. Establishing this bond is akin to drawing spiritual nourishment from a wellspring of grace. Her messages, often marked by urgency yet suffused with hope, implore us to adopt these daily practices as means of grace, paths that perpetuate our journey into deeper holiness and divine intimacy.

In essence, these daily practices rooted in Medjugorje's messages and mirrored in the teachings of the Church set a rhythm that attunes our lives to divine harmony. They remind us that spiritual growth is an unfolding journey, a continual metamorphosis shaped by actions as much as by faith. Such practices serve as spiritual anchors, grounding believers in the eternal truths of faith and filling each day with renewed purpose.

Ultimately, these daily practices for spiritual growth aren't burdens to bear but blessings to cherish. They align us with God's will, ensuring that each step, every prayer, and all moments of reflection craft a pathway to a life rich with peace, purpose, and divine love. Through embracing these spiritual practices, we heed the call from Our Lady, transforming our lives into reflections of heavenly grace, a testament to the sacred messages heralding from Medjugorje.

Implementing Instructions in Modern Life

The timeless messages from Our Lady of Medjugorje resonate with a simple yet profound call: to anchor our lives in prayer and faith, amidst the cacophony of modern existence. In a world often overshadowed by chaos and distractions, these instructions serve as a beacon, guiding us back to the essence of our spiritual journey. The true challenge lies not merely in understanding these messages but in weaving them into the fabric of our daily lives, allowing them to transform ordinary routines into extraordinary encounters with the divine.

Our Lady's messages are calls to action, urging us to rekindle practices that might seem archaic to the modern secular mind—fasting, prayer, and contemplation. Yet, in adopting these practices, the faithful don't retreat from the world; rather, they engage more profoundly with it. Fasting, for instance, is not just an abstention from food; it's an invitation to detach from and transcend material distractions, focusing our attention and energy on spiritual nourishment. By integrating fasting into modern life as a regular practice, people open up a space within themselves for divine grace to manifest, enabling clearer discernment and a deeper connection to God.

Incorporating daily prayer into a bustling schedule may appear daunting, yet Our Lady emphasizes its vital role in securing inner peace. Imagine starting every day by tuning into a divine frequency, where prayer acts as the dial that removes static and enhances clarity of life's purpose. a short morning prayer or mid-day pause for the Angelus can provide anchor points in the chaos of daily responsibilities. These brief moments serve as gentle reminders that God is ever-present, reorienting our focus from worldly concerns to heavenly promises.

As much as Our Lady's messages encourage individual commitment to spiritual disciplines, they also call us to community—a compelling antidote to the sense of isolation that plagues many in contemporary society. Implementing these instructions collectively in families and communities can reinvigorate familial bonds and strengthen communal spirit. Consider the power of the family rosary, as it pulls together the strands of individual lives, uniting them in a shared rhythm of prayer, thereby cultivating an environment where faith is not just professed but lived out in unity and love.

The emphasis on peace is perhaps one of the most pertinent instructions for today's world. The call to peace extends beyond personal tranquility; it is a mission, a conscious endeavor to be peace-bearers in our environments. It challenges us to practice forgiveness, to sow understanding where discord exists, and to become channels of peace within our spheres of influence. By practicing peace, we embody the message of Medjugorje in every interaction, allowing our lived spirituality to inspire more than mere personal transformation—it becomes a catalyst for societal change.

But what of the demands and constraints of a modern lifestyle that seem incongruent with such spiritual exercises? It is here that the instructions shine most brightly, urging us not toward withdrawal, but toward an enlightened engagement. Let the workplace, the home, and public spaces become venues where divine love is both expressed and experienced. Such transformation begins not in monumental acts, but in conscious daily choices: extending kindness, acting justly, and walking humbly with God. As these choices accumulate, they generate a ripple effect, eventually altering the atmosphere of the environments in which we dwell.

For the messages to truly take root, it's essential that they seep into not just our routines but our very essence, shaping our thoughts, actions, and intentions. This becomes a lifelong endeavor, requiring persistence and conscious effort. The saints of old remind us that holiness is not achieved through grand gestures but through daily fidelity and perseverance in spiritual disciplines. In modern life, practice patience as you allow these disciplines to cultivate a garden of virtues within you that blossoms in due time, bearing witness to the transformative power of our Lady's instructions.

Moreover, these instructions are not confined to personal spiritual growth; they have vast implications for evangelization. By living out these messages authentically, the faithful naturally become witnesses to the truth and beauty of their faith. Witnessing is not about preaching but embodying the gospel in such a way that others are drawn to understand the source of one's peace and joy. It's about being living testimonies of the love of God, as demonstrated through our deeds and the serene strength we exude even amidst life's tempests.

In the end, implementing these sacred instructions in modern life is akin to embarking on a pilgrimage—a spiritual journey that transforms the mundane into the mystic. Whether through fasting that purifies intentions, prayer that aligns our will with God's, or acts of peace that ripple through communities, these practices equip us to be the custodians of joy and bearers of a hope that transcends the transient sufferings of this world. Thus, the messages of Medjugorje are not relics of past apparitions but living words that beckon us to forge a path to holiness in the here and now. They remind us that this path, though challenging, is paved with grace, leading us to an eternal destiny filled with divine love and communion.

Chapter 13: Analyzing the Messages Comprensively

In this chapter, we delve into the profound depths of the messages from Medjugorje, engaging with them not merely as mystical communications but as treasures of spiritual guidance, necessitating a discerning eye. We embark on an exploration that requires both faith and reason, striving to connect each message with the enduring truths found in Sacred Scripture and the rich history of Sacred Tradition. To truly comprehend the divine whispers of Our Lady, one must utilize a balanced methodology, blending scriptural exegesis with an appreciation for the spiritual context of contemporary times. This endeavor is marked by a quest for consistency and integrity within the messages, carefully evaluating their alignment with the Church's teachings and their resonance in the hearts of the faithful. Presented with a fabric woven with celestial intent, our task is to discern its patterns amid the chaos of the world, extracting from it a roadmap that leads us closer to the divine heart. Through this analysis, we unveil layers of divine communication aimed at transformation, offering us a path to both personal sanctity and communal peace, as we seek to faithfully live out the profound call presented to us.

Methods to Analyze Spiritual Messages

Understanding and interpreting spiritual messages from Medjugorje involves a discerning journey, one that requires the heart as much as the mind. The process of analysis here is not purely academic; it is an intricate dance between faith and reason. First, we must recognize the significance of context—both historical and spiritual—in analyzing these messages. The roots of Medjugorje's messages intertwine deeply with the traditions of Roman Catholicism, revealing a vibrant heirloom where divine whispers echo through sacred texts and human history alike.

Historical context opens a window into understanding the circumstances surrounding the apparitions. By analyzing the socio-political environment of early Medjugorje, we unearth the soil from which these spiritual roots have grown. The apparitions began in the turbulence of 1981, a period marked by geopolitical uncertainties. Yet amidst this chaos, messages of peace and hope emerged, resonating deeply with the universal cry for divine intervention. Such contextual comprehension allows scholars and believers alike to discern patterns and detect any divergences from established Church teachings.

Furthermore, a methodical approach requires comparing the messages to Sacred Scripture and Sacred Tradition, serving as the foundation upon which the Catholic faith is constructed. The task here is akin to weaving a tapestry, where each thread must align harmoniously with the others to convey a coherent narrative. The messages are examined for theological consistency, scrutinizing whether they reflect Christological truths upheld by the Church for millennia. Are these messages calling us to deeper communion with God, echoing the teachings of Christ Himself? This alignment often reveals the divine harmony, serving as a beacon for the faithful.

The role of ecclesiastical authority cannot be understated in this process. The Church, with her wisdom and experience, acts as the guiding light, discerning the authenticity of revelations. The processes established by the Magisterium—meticulous, vigilant, and rooted in tradition—are essential in safeguarding the faithful from theological error. This adds a level of credibility that must be respected, for in matters of spirituality, a balance between skepticism and belief is necessary for a mature faith.

To further strengthen analysis, engaging with the testimonies of those transformed by these messages becomes invaluable. Personal stories—of conversions, healings, and the rekindling of faith—add a human element to the spiritual discourse. These narratives, filled with passion and divine encounters, create an emotional connect that transcends mere doctrinal validation. They are not only evidence but also living manifestations of the messages' power, acting as spiritual bridges that connect individual experiences with the collective faith journey.

It is equally important to employ a philosophical lens, embracing wisdom from thinkers across ages. Philosophical inquiry into the nature of truth, belief, and divine revelation can offer fresh insights into interpreting these spiritual missives. Can we discern the divine language through our limited human perspective, or is there an instinctual resonance that guides us toward understanding? Philosophy encourages us to question while remaining open to the mysteries that lie beyond comprehension.

Moreover, prayer and reflection form the heart of analyzing these messages. It's in the quiet moments of contemplation that hidden meanings reveal themselves, as if whispered by the wind's breath. Prayer aligns us with God's heart, attuning our spirit to divine frequencies. Through earnest supplication and meditation, we invite divine wisdom to shine light on paths otherwise obscured by human bias or misunderstanding.

In these analyses, there is no room for manipulation or distortion of truths. Honesty and humility are virtues that guide this scholarly pilgrimage. If interpretations deviate from the central truths of faith, they must be reexamined and understood anew. The call is for purity of heart and clarity of thought, echoing the Beatitudes, where the pure shall see God.

These methods to analyze spiritual messages are not exhaustive, for the divine mystery is inexhaustible in its richness and depth. The journey is not merely academic but experiential, transforming the seeker in the process. It is an invitation to explore, to question, and to embrace the unknown with a heart full of faith and a mind eager to learn. As we delve deeper into the messages of Medjugorje, we not only seek understanding but find ourselves dancing on the edge of the eternal, where faith meets revelation and heaven touches earth.

Evaluating the Consistency and Integrity

The messages from Medjugorje invite an earnest exploration into their consistency and integrity. This task, much like combing through a profound spiritual system, demands patience and discernment. The seers, simple vessels through whom the divine purportedly speaks, articulate messages that are meant to align with the rich traditions and texts of Catholicism. Yet this alignment cannot be taken at face value. It requires a meticulous examination to ensure that what is being communicated not only harmonizes with established dogma but also imbues it with renewed vitality.

The heart of this evaluation lies in comparing the messages with the Sacred Tradition and Sacred Scripture. There must be a seamless integration between the words of the seers and the teachings that have been revered for centuries. Catholicism does not shy away from its history, standing strong with its foundations. Thus, consistency means more than mere repetition; it's an unfolding, where each message becomes a continuation of a divine dialogue that spans millennia. The integrity, then, is found in this unbroken thread – a testament to the authenticity of these messages.

Consistent messages are often those that resonate with the core tenets of the faith: love, peace, and repentance. Yet, it's not only about abstract principles; it's the ways in which these principles are woven into the narrative and guidance provided by the seers. Are they urging the faithful toward actions and reflections that honor the spirit of Christianity? Are they manifesting in ways that are both timely and timeless, connecting past wisdom with present lives?

This brings us to the issue of integrity. Integrity in divine messages means they must be coherent, truthful, and edifying. Consider integrity as the backbone of these revelations; it strengthens the message, making it robust enough to withstand scrutiny. A message's integrity is often judged by its fruit – does it promote a more profound conversion, a deeper peace, a stronger faith?

In our evaluation, we must also look at whether these messages possess a certain transparency. Are they open to interpretation within the framework of tradition and scripture? For any message claiming divine origin, there cannot be ambiguity that leads followers astray. Integrity demands clarity and comprehension, catered to the spiritual needs of the faithful.

Moreover, evaluating these messages' consistency and integrity involves listening to the echoes of similar revelations throughout church history. The apparitions at Medjugorje aren't isolated phenomena. They find parallels in Lourdes, Fatima, and other significant Marian apparitions. Each of these occurrences presents an opportunity to cross-reference themes and instructions, creating a mosaic that reflects the continuity of Mary's guidance across different eras and cultures.

Any deviation from this established narrative must be carefully discerned. While the messages bring new insights, they should never contradict the fundamentals of faith. Here is where theological scholars and devout laity join forces. Their interpretation and understanding bring a shared wisdom crucial for evaluating these sacred messages.

Furthermore, personal testimonies play an invaluable role. The Medjugorje narratives have inspired many individuals towards conversion and renewal of faith. Thus, it's pertinent to gather these testimonies to assess whether such transformations reflect a genuine response to the messages' intent and content.

The approach to evaluating consistency and integrity must be both intellectual and spiritual. Embracing prayer and reflection while engaging in rigorous academic scrutiny creates a balanced approach. It bridges the divine with human discernment, ensuring that integrity is not sacrificed to blind faith or skepticism.

In conclusion, assessing the consistency and integrity of Medjugorje's messages encompasses more than historical or textual analysis. It's about tracing the divine fingerprint through various expressions of faith across different contexts. The real measure of these messages lies in their ability to sustain, nurture, and grow the Catholic faiths's luminous tradition. Only by upholding this scrutiny can we appreciate these messages as heavenly dialogs meant to fortify and renew the Church's mission on Earth.

Chapter 14: Creating Medjugorje Prayers

In the sacred and serene endeavor of crafting prayers inspired by the messages of Medjugorje, one unveils not just words, but a system built with heavenly intention that connects believers to the divine. These prayers, born from the profound encounters with Our Lady, serve as both a beacon and a bridge, guiding each soul towards deeper communion with God. Rooted in the rich soil of scripture and tradition, the prayers reflect the simple yet boundless hope of Medjugorje's apparitions. Here, the light of faith shines through, illuminating the pilgrim's path with grace and undying love. Each utterance becomes a vessel, carrying the faithful closer to the heart of Jesus, while echoing the celestial harmony of peace that transcends the earthly realm. As prayer interlaces with the daily rhythm of life, it transforms the believer's journey into an ever-unfolding story of divine love and spiritual renewal, calling all to embrace the transcendent mystery with open hearts and unwavering devotion.

Crafting Prayers Inspired by Medjugorje

The journey to crafting prayers inspired by Medjugorje begins with a sincere desire to connect with the divine messages that have been imparted through the visions of the seers. These prayers are born from a place of deep contemplation and an earnest yearning to emulate the spirit of the messages received. In Medjugorje, the Virgin Mary is said to have appeared, reminding the faithful of the virtues of peace, love, and repentance. Her calls have become a gentle yet persistent echo within the hearts of many believers. They draw us towards a prayerful life, inviting us to weave these messages into our spiritual dialogue with God.

Creating a prayer deeply influenced by the messages of Medjugorje requires more than mere adherence to words. It demands immersion into the essence of the messages. When considering the visions of Medjugorje, there's an undeniable infusion of maternal warmth and a call to return to sacred simplicity. The seers often speak of Mary's call to renew one's faith through daily prayer. In this sacred practice, one discovers that words alone don't complete a prayer; it's the heart's intent and the soul's openness that truly imbue it with power.

In the art of crafting these prayers, inspiration can be drawn from various elements of the Medjugorje experience. Consider the emphasis on peace—a recurring theme that Mary emphasizes. A prayer rooted in peace becomes a sanctuary, inviting both the supplicant and the divine presence into a tranquil dialogue. Imagine your words as gentle ripples in a pond, expanding outward, calling forth a peace that transcends human understanding. "O Queen of Peace, sow in our hearts the seeds of your eternal peace, that we may become instruments of God's love in this troubled world," one might begin. This simple invocation sets a tone of harmony that's inextricably linked to Medjugorje's core messages.

Additionally, humility and surrender are key characteristics illustrated in the messages of Medjugorje. The crafting of a prayer can also embody these virtues. Just as Mary humbly accepted her role as the Mother of God, we are encouraged to offer our lives and petitions to God with a humble spirit. A Medjugorje-inspired prayer might thus include words of surrender: "Lord, I lay before You my fears and desires; take them, mold them, that I may walk in your light, trusting in Your divine providence."

Reflecting on personal moments of conversion is another powerful way to personalize prayers from Medjugorje. The apparitions often spark profound transformation, leading many to reflect on their own paths of faith. A prayer could capture the essence of conversion by requesting divine grace to continually turn toward God: "Heavenly Father, like the pilgrims of Medjugorje, let my heart be ever mutable, ever open to Your call, that I may find new life in Your promise."

Moreover, the messages from Medjugorje advocate for the family as a cornerstone of faith, suggesting that prayers be crafted as collective invocations of grace. A family prayer might begin with a request for unity, invoking blessings over the household: "Blessed Mother, we knit ourselves together in prayer, seeking your guidance and protection for our loved ones. May our home be a beacon of your peace and love."

The vibrant deposit of Medjugorje's teachings also encourages one to dialogue with scripture when composing prayers. The messages often align harmoniously with biblical tenets, which can be intricately woven into the fabric of prayer. Recall how familiar biblical imagery, like the Good Shepherd or the Prodigal Son, resonates with Mary's calls for deeper conversion and fidelity. Prayers that echo these narratives can deepen our relationship with God and the Holy Trinity.

True to the allegorical nature of the messages, a Medjugorje-inspired prayer can also employ vivid imagery to move the soul. Picture the image of the Virgin, standing amidst a rain of stars, hands outstretched in a gesture of invitation and grace. One might pen: "O Immaculate Heart of Mary, like the stars that guide the weary traveler, illuminate our paths with your gentle love, leading us to safe harbors in divine mercy."

In the ebb and flow of daily life, such prayers don't just mark isolated moments of contemplation but can become the rhythm by which our lives are measured. The Mother of Medjugorje invites us not just to recite these devotions but to embody them, creating a living prayer through our actions. It's in the small acts of kindness and in the compassion we show to others that these prayers reach their fulfillment.

Ultimately, crafting Medjugorje prayers is an exercise in simplicity and truth. It's paving a path back to the heart of the Christian tradition, where prayer is a living, breathing testament to our faith. In every word and every breath, let us draw nearer to the heart of Mary, and through her, to the heart of God. This is the sacred art of Medjugorje-inspired prayers—an art crafted not merely by human hands, but guided by heavenly inspiration.

As you engage in this sacred act, know that these prayers, humble and heartfelt, are parts in the grand design of divine conversation. They are, indeed, offerings that stretch beyond the confines of time and space, bridging heaven and earth, bringing our hopes, dreams, and sorrows before the Almighty. In the serene embrace of Medjugorje's messages, may you find your voice, whispering your truths and receiving heavenly peace in return.

Sample Prayers to Our Lady

In the quiet moments of devotion, we turn our thoughts to the Queen of Peace, Our Lady of Medjugorje. It is through her messages and manifestations that the spiritual life takes on a profound clarity. The seers of Medjugorje, touched by her radiant presence, have been blessed to share heavenly insights, which have ignited hearts and minds across the globe. As we contemplate the richness of these revelations, it becomes fitting to enter into prayer, a channel through which we can express our love, gratitude, and supplications. These prayers to Our Lady act as bridges between earth and the divine, tokens of our desire to align our worldly lives with celestial aspirations.

One might start with a prayer of thanksgiving—a simple yet deeply felt acknowledgment of the Virgin's presence in our lives. "O tender Mother, we thank you for the grace of your visits, for filling our hearts with peace and trust. Through your gentle guidance, may we walk the path of holiness and embrace the life of faith." This prayer invites us to reflect on the blessings that descend upon us through her intercessions, encouraging a spirit of gratitude which transforms our daily engagements into acts of worship.

Another vital prayer centers on the theme of peace, a core message from Medjugorje. "Our Lady of Peace, enfold our troubled world in your mantle of serenity. Inspire leaders to seek justice and compassion, and bring harmony to fractured souls. Within our hearts, cultivate the lasting peace that springs from Christ's love." Here, we not only beseech peace in the global context but also recognize our personal need for inner tranquility, urging us to become instruments of peace in our own communities.

An unparalleled call echoed from Medjugorje is the devotion to consistent prayer, particularly through the Rosary. A prayer aligned with this theme might be: "Queen of the Rosary, aid us in our devotion, as each bead passed through our fingers draws us closer to your Son. May our recitations be a symphony of love that echoes through our souls and echoes into eternity." By engaging in this meditative prayer practice, we experience the profound introspection and communion with the divine that the Rosary offers, affirming our connection to both Our Lady and her Son, Jesus Christ.

In penning these prayers, we must remember that they are not mere words, but powerful invocations, steeped in faith and tradition. They allow us to participate in a sacred dialogue, an expression of our innermost hopes and fears laid bare before our heavenly Mother. Each word is chosen with the reverence and contemplation befitting such an august occasion.

Prayers for strength and courage fill another essential space. "O Mary, Most Pure, in moments of trial and tribulation, lend us your strength. May your unwavering faith be our fortress, your boundless love our shield. Guide our steps as we navigate the hardships of life, finding solace in your maternal care." This intention extends beyond personal resilience, fostering a communal shield that supports and uplifts those who might falter, embodying the shared mission of mercy and compassion that Our Lady encourages.

For those undergoing conversion, a prayer for openness to transformation is a sacred step on their spiritual journey. "Mother of Conversion, open our hearts to God's boundless love. Break the chains of sin that bind us and lead us to the light of your Son's salvation. May our renewed spirits become beacons of hope for others." In aligning ourselves with this calling, we echo the very heart of Medjugorje's messages—turning towards God with a humble openness to His transformative power.

Contemplating on Our Lady's call to live a life imbued with faith, a prayer for deepened faith could be: "Virgin Mary, you who believed, teach us to trust amidst our doubts. Strengthen our faith, that it might be as the rock upon which our lives are built. In every moment of despair, remind us of the victory of your Son's Resurrection, and guide us through the valleys to new heights of understanding." Through this prayer, we encourage an ever-closer relationship with the divine, one that remains steadfast amidst the trials of earthly existence.

It's important to appreciate that these prayers are not static or formulaic; rather, they are living, breathing expressions of our continuous journey of faith. Engaging with them daily molds our spiritual life, transforming our mundane routines into sacred rhythms of grace and intention.

In closing our reflections on these prayers, it is evident that they serve as powerful conduits through which we can continually foster our relationship with Our Lady and, by extension, with God. They echo the sentiments found in Sacred Tradition and Scripture while responding to the unique messages of Medjugorje. Embraced with a sincere heart, these spiritual dialogues propel us forward, ushering in a new dawn of divine love and understanding in our lives. May we always find solace and inspiration in Our Lady's embrace, as we aspire to a life marked by devotion and holiness.

Chapter 15: Meditational Insights from Medjugorje

In the tranquil embrace of Medjugorje, believers find an opus of meditational practices interconnected with Divine messages that thrum with the cadence of biblical wisdom. This sacred location unravels a mystical path to deeper devotion, compelling us to silence the mind and open the heart to the celestial whispers that flutter through the air with each pilgrimage. Here, amidst rolling hills and gentle breezes, the meditative practices echoed in the very stones guide the faithful to a profound dialogue with the Divine—an encounter that beckons reflection not only on the ethereal messages of Our Lady but also on the scriptural truths that underpin Christian faith. By uniting ancient biblical passages with fresh revelations, these practices draw upon centuries-old traditions, creating a harmonious symphony of quiet contemplation and active faith. Thus, Medjugorje stands as a living testament, where meditation becomes a vessel for transformation, whispering the timeless truths of heaven's promise through the gentle rhythm of prayerful silence and steadfast reflection.

Meditative Practices for Devotion

The embrace of meditative practices as a path to devotion finds profound resonance within the spiritual landscape of Medjugorje. Here, amidst the hills and sanctuaries, pilgrims are invited not just to witness divine apparitions but to enter into a deeper communion with the sacred. The meditative practices emerging from Medjugorje blend the heart's yearning with the soul's ascent, crafting a holistic journey that elevates their devotion to new spiritual heights.

Central to these practices is the rosary, a spiritual anchor for many believers. The rosary serves as a rhythmic meditation, each bead a stepping stone into deeper layers of contemplation and prayer. By recounting the life of Christ through the mysteries, devotees transcend mere recitation, entering into a living prayer that infuses their meditative moments with the presence of the divine. As they turn each bead, they simultaneously insert their lives into Sacred Tradition.

The rosary's role in meditation is complemented by the presence of silence, often emphasized in Medjugorje's messages. Silence is more than a mere absence of noise; it's a profound presence that allows the soul to discern whispers of divine love. In the quiet of one's heart, amidst the gentle rustle of nature or within the hallowed walls of a chapel, silence emerges as a conduit through which divine insights flow. Medjugorje inspires believers to embrace silence, fostering spaces where God's voice can echo unimpeded in their hearts.

An integral aspect of meditative devotion also lies in scriptural reflection. Medjugorje's messages often intertwine with biblical themes, encouraging a contemplative study of scripture. This practice allows individuals to dwell on passages that illuminate their path, imbuing their meditation with the wisdom and guidance embedded within sacred text. By aligning their personal experiences with biblical narratives, meditatees draw strength from the eternal truths of faith and divine grace.

At the heart of Medjugorje's call to deepened meditation is a renewed understanding of the Eucharist. Here lies a profound invitation to enter into the mystery of Christ's presence in the bread and wine. Meditative adoration before the Blessed Sacrament becomes a transformative encounter, where the boundaries between heaven and earth blur. The Eucharist compels the believer into a silent dialogue of love, gratitude, and surrender, making this sacramental encounter a cornerstone of Medjugorje's spiritual heritage.

Fasting, traditionally viewed within Medjugorje as a tool for spiritual purification, also plays a vital role in meditative devotion. When combined with prayer, fasting enhances clarity of mind and spirit, uniting body and soul in a singular act of worship. This harmonious interweaving of physical and spiritual disciplines deepens the individual's meditative experience, purifying intention and drawing the practitioner closer to God.

Furthermore, the pilgrimage itself is a living form of meditation. Traversing the hallowed landscapes of Medjugorje, pilgrims physically and spiritually journey towards the divine. Each step, each prayer whispered into the wind is an invitation to draw nearer to Our Lady and her Son. This act of pilgrimage becomes a metaphorical journey, allowing one to leave the mundane behind and seek the sacred with renewed purpose and devotion.

The dynamic of community meditation in Medjugorje should not be underestimated. While individual prayer remains central, gathering in communal reflection creates a synergy of shared faith and mutual support. This shared space amplifies the meditative experience, drawing individuals into a collective heartbeat of prayer and devotion. The palpable presence of collective intention transforms personal meditation into a divine fellowship.

Encompassing these practices is a gentler examen of conscience, where the soul reflects upon its journey, seeking illumination of spiritual progress and hidden shadows. Medjugorje's messages call for inward introspection as a pathway to holiness, urging believers to view their lives through the lens of divine mercy and light.

Ultimately, Medjugorje's meditative practices for devotion transcend mere routine; they ignite a yearning for deeper intimacy with God. They encourage a continual ascent toward the divine, fostering a sacred space where the soul can breathe the breath of eternity. In embracing these practices, devotees open themselves to a profound encounter with the divine Mother and her Son, journeying ever closer to the heartbeat of heaven.

Reflecting on Messages and Biblical Passages

The marriage of the divine inspirations from Medjugorje with the rich history of biblical passages offers a profound canvas for contemplation. These divine messages serve as luminous threads, weaving through the fabric of sacred scripture, illuminating its timeless truths with fresh vitality. As we embark on this journey of reflection, we delve deep into the resonance between the celestial communications given through the seers and the biblical narratives beloved by so many across generations.

What strikes at the heart of these Medjugorje messages is their profound alignment with the virtues extolled in the Gospel. Consider, for instance, the repeated call for peace—a theme that echoes Christ's call for peace throughout his ministry. "Peace I leave with you, my peace I give to you," he tenderly spoke in the Upper Room, words that reverberate across centuries and find a living echo in the gentle urging of Our Lady of Medjugorje. The messages serve as a clarion call, urging all to seek that inner tranquility born of faith.

This harmony between the messages and biblical teachings does more than merely corroborate their heavenly origin; it underscores the eternal nature of divine love and wisdom. In much the same way, the call to fasting from the Medjugorje messages parallels the exhortations seen in the Hebrew Scriptures. Fasting, a symbolic act of surrender and devotion, serves not just as an ancient tradition but as a living practice, inviting the faithful to emulate the austerity of the prophets and embrace a life of humble reverence.

One cannot ignore the allegorical richness imbued in the messages of Medjugorje. Much like the parables of old, they operate on multiple levels, inviting a spectrum of interpretations and reflections. "Repent and believe in the Gospel," resonate the shadows of John the Baptist's cry, mirrored yet again in these private revelations, urging a return to the heart of the Christian message. Such echoes act as divine signposts, directing us back to the source—the Word made flesh, who dwelt among us.

Through the meditative practice of aligning Medjugorje's messages with scripture, we find a symphony of divine interaction. Indeed, Mary's role as a guiding presence is reinforced by her unwavering consistency with Christ's teachings and her own scriptural life. Her messages' simplicity and clarity remind us of the Beatitudes—the blessings that offer a roadmap to holiness. We are called to embody a righteousness that surpasses mere observance, reaching into the depths of compassionate action and genuine faith.

The allegorical landscape of Medjugorje's insights breathes life into the stories of our ancestors in faith. Such reflections beckon us to view ourselves as part of a grand narrative, where the voice of God continues to speak through the halls of time. As students of scripture and souls on a pilgrim path, we are drawn to revisit the messages that — like the luminescence of stars — guide travelers on a shadowed road. Through contemplation of these divine revelations and their scriptural resonances, we find ourselves situated not between years, but between eternity and now.

A rich aspect of this reflective process is understanding how the messages challenge us to renew our commitment to living a life of holiness and service. Medjugorje's insistence on prayer reflects the Psalms' ancient call: "Be still, and know that I am God." Within these parallels lies the universal invitation to discover the sacred quietude amid life's clamor. Here, every whisper of prayer becomes an echo of devotion, a testament to the transformative power imbued in faith-filled petitions.

Furthermore, the repeated emphasis on community and unity in these messages finds its biblical counterpart in the Acts of the Apostles. The early Church's communal living inspires contemporary reflection on how unity can foster spiritual growth and echo the divine unity in the Trinity. Medjugorje's messages become more than a call to personal conversion; they rise to a collective demand for solidarity and compassion among believers worldwide.

Therefore, as we dissect these insights within a meditative framework, we uncover a treasure trove of wisdom and spiritual discernment. Each message, when held up to the light of scripture, glows with insight and direction, shaping the path toward spiritual maturity. In holding scripture as both mirror and map, the messages of Medjugorje help re-engage our hearts with biblical principles, casting our contemporary journey in the archetypal light. This, in turn, continues to mold a generation of believers committed to embodying Christ's love in an ever-changing world.

When we consider these reflections, we allow the spirit of discernment to flourish amidst our sacred traditions and daily life. The divine interplay between Medjugorje's heavenly voices and the biblical word remains a testament to God's unchanging love—a beacon that guides, renews, and challenges us to deeper truths.

In our contemplation, we embrace the timeless reality of Christ's words made manifest in modern revelations, reminding us of the unending dialogue between heaven and earth. This contemplative fusion serves as an invitation to engage with the sacred mysteries, where the messages of Medjugorje become both harp and hymn, evoking praise from the deepest recesses of the soul.

Chapter 16: Reflections on Marian Devotion

The warm expression of Marian devotion, intricately woven through centuries of faith and fervor, invites us to pause and ponder its essence in our lives today. In Medjugorje, the call to turn our hearts towards Mary is not merely an invitation but a pilgrimage to a deeper understanding of love and grace bestowed upon humanity. The tender messages from these apparitions call the faithful to a profound communion with Our Lady, echoing the timeless chorus of hope and intercession. Engaging with Marian devotion is an exploration of dual mysteries—the mystery of our faith and the mystery of God's unyielding love expressed through Our Lady's guidance. This devotion does not draw us away from Christ but, like threads in a majestic legacy, brings us ever closer to Him by walking in the rhythm of Mary's heart—her humility, her obedience, her unwavering faith. As we reflect on the beauty and significance of Marian devotion, we find it harmoniously aligned with Sacred Tradition and Sacred Scripture, an eternal whisper calling us each day to a sacred space of peace and reflection.

The Significance of Marian Devotion Today

Marian devotion, timeless and profound, continues to hold an essential place in the heart of the Roman Catholic Church. In today's chaotic world, where the clamor of modern living frequently drowns out whispers of the divine, devotion to Mary offers a natural anchor, a reminder of serene faith and maternal comfort. This practice is not just an echo of bygone days; it speaks directly to contemporary struggles, needs, and aspirations, aligning beautifully with the lessons endowed by Medjugorje's visionaries. Their experiences and revelations have intensified the global consciousness of Mary's ongoing role, illuminating her as a beacon of hope and intercession.

Our Lady's messages in Medjugorje reveal a layered opus of spiritual guidance, each thread woven with intent and divine purpose. In a world often characterized by disconnection and discord, the call to Marian devotion is a summons back to spiritual cohesion and peace. Her messages emphasize core tenets of the faith—prayer, peace, and conversion—each serving as a pillar for transforming personal lives and communities. The immediacy of these messages ensures they resonate deeply with Catholics, instilling a sense of purpose that transcends ordinary life.

Delving into Marian devotion is like embarking on a journey where the soul rediscovers its roots. It provides a sanctuary where believers can encounter an intimate relationship with Jesus through His mother. This relationship fosters a profound sense of spiritual intimacy, offering solace that is as tender as it is transformative. For many, Mary's presence is akin to a loving guide, leading them toward a greater understanding of themselves and their faith.

Why is Marian devotion crucial today? It serves as a spiritual counterpoint to secular narratives, advocating for values not always championed by modern society. Her messages are timely reminders to cherish simplicity, humility, and compassion. In reflecting on Marian devotion, we are reminded that each act of faith and prayer contributes to the edifice of the Church, strengthening the global Catholic community.

The rosary, a quintessential practice of Marian devotion, exemplifies a meditative journey through the life of Christ—a journey that invites introspection and divine encounter. The repetitive nature of the prayer cultivates a tranquil space, a rhythm that calms the mind and heart, encouraging deeper reflection on the mysteries of life. This practice aligns seamlessly with the messages of Medjugorje, which prioritize prayer as both a personal and communal bridge to spiritual rejuvenation.

Contributing to its enduring appeal, Marian devotion answers a universal call for peace. In the face of societal unrest and inner turmoil, Mary's messages of peace resonate with an unequivocal power. She invites us to become vessels of peace, urging transformation that reaches beyond personal boundaries. Marian devotion thus forms the bedrock of spiritual activism, where the act of following Mary's example becomes an effort to heal the world's fractures.

The legacy of Medjugorje's messages enhances the relevance of Marian devotion, affirming its harmony with sacred tradition and scripture. They are threads in the fabric of Catholic heritage, a testament to the continuity of Marian influence throughout ages. Devotion to Mary fosters a unity that transcends individual faith experiences, binding the collective spirit of the Church in shared love and reverence.

Moreover, Marian devotion extends a universal invitation—not limited to Catholics alone, but to all who seek divine wisdom. It is a spiritual conduit through which God's grace flows, offering profound insight and comfort to those who open their hearts to it. Why does this matter so much today? Because in the hearts of believers, the gentle call of Mary echoes the eternal call of God, nourishing a faith that is both ancient and ever new.

Through Marian devotion, Catholics around the world find a powerful means to embody their faith actively. It nurtures the virtues that are central to Christian life—love for God, selfless care for others, and a profound commitment to spiritual growth. The Church, through Mary's devotion, continues to thrive, offering a roadmap to holiness that is paved with her intercessory power and motherly guidance.

One cannot underestimate the allegorical lessons present in Mary's life and their relevance to modern believers. Her humility, obedience, and courage speak volumes, offering an aspirational model that is profoundly relatable yet infinitely divine. In embodying these virtues, Marian devotion extends beyond mere admiration and enters the realm of actionable faith—a faith that encourages believers to lead lives reflecting her radiant light.

Mary's presence in the lives of the faithful as depicted in Medjugorje transcends the dichotomy between sacred and mundane. Her messages transform ordinary moments into opportunities for reflection and prayer, blending spiritual discipline with daily life. This integrated approach inspires a holistic spirituality, one that embraces both the divine and the human in every aspect of life.

In conclusion, the significance of Marian devotion today is vast and multi-faceted, a treasure trove of spiritual richness awaiting those who seek it. As we reflect upon the insights brought forth from Medjugorje, let us recognize the pivotal role that Mary continues to play in guiding the faithful toward fuller participation in their spiritual lives. Her message is timeless, and its call to prayer, peace, and personal conversion is as urgent now as ever.

Personal Reflections and Insights

In tracing the history of Marian devotion woven through the annals of Medjugorje's significance, one finds a moment of profound introspection. The stories of visions and messages, experienced by the seers, invite us to pause and reflect on the depth of our own faith journey. What does it mean to truly embrace Marian devotion in our own lives? This question does not merely ask us to follow blindly but calls us to probe deeply into our own souls, to uncover the mysteries that linger just beyond the surface of everyday life.

Consider the symbolism encased in the image of the Madonna. She is portrayed across cultures and epochs as a beacon of hope, a font of wisdom, and a source of divine intercession. This enduring image speaks to a universal longing—a yearning for a maternal presence that nurtures both the communal and individual aspects of our spiritual lives. Mary's role as a mediator between humanity and the divine provides each of us a pathway to understand our own capacity for love, sacrifice, and faith. The messages from Medjugorje underscore this, offering modern followers the comfort that the Eternal Mother is listening, guiding us ever closer to her Son.

Devotion to Mary is not just remembering her maternal love; it's also engaging with her teachings in a way that transforms our lives. These encounters with the divine often echo Jesus' earthy ministry, reminding us that spirituality is not only an act of contemplation but also an urgent call to justice and service in the world. Mary's messages might reach us through the lens of the seers of Medjugorje, but they reflect timeless truths that lift our spirits and challenge our souls to embrace a fuller expression of love and compassion.

Through the narratives and teachings of Mary, we engage in a spiritual dialogue that extends beyond the dimensions of time and place. In each rosary we recite, each Hail Mary that passes through our lips, there lies an invocation of connection—a tether not only to the divine but to each other. It's an invitation to participate in the sacred mysteries of life, to transcend our mundane existence and glimpse the extraordinary nature of our calling. These prayerful moments are opportunities to see the divine present in our everyday struggles and triumphs.

Yet, understanding Marian devotion in the context of Medjugorje also prompts us to consider our roles as participants in this unfolding story. The teachings presented here do not exist in a vacuum but call us to act, to be the hands and feet of Christ in the world. The commitment of faith reflected in Mary's messages urges a transformation from passive observance to active faith—a kind of faith that can move mountains and change hearts. We are beckoned to embody the grace and virtues that Mary herself exemplifies: humility, purity, compassion, and unwavering faith.

As we delve deeper into personal insights, we face the realities of modern life that sometimes dim the clarity of divine revelations. This duality—the sacred and the profane—underscores a tension that believers seeking greater devotion must navigate. Through reflection, the messages of Medjugorje challenge us to mediate this tension, finding harmony between spiritual aspirations and worldly duties. In doing so, we learn to carry the sanctuary within ourselves, allowing divine light to illuminate our paths and instill peace in the chaos of our everyday existence.

These reflections also prompt us to question the nature of faith itself. True devotion isn't confined to a set of ritually conducted prayers or visits to sanctuaries. Rather, it calls for a transformation that is intimate and profound, something that renews our spirit daily. The essence of Marian devotion, distilled through Medjugorje, becomes a guide, harmonizing with the sacred music of our lives. With each step forward, our faith matures, growing resilient and steadfast.

In observing the personal narratives of those who have devoted themselves to Marian spirituality, we find a system of lived experiences that magnify this divine maternal presence. These stories resonate with evidence of profound connection, hope, and transformation. They whisper of encounters that reignite the flames of faith, urging us to emulate the unwavering faithfulness of Mary. Through these reflections, we are reminded that Mary's call is not just for the select few but an invitation extended to all humankind—a call to grow in love and reflect divinity in our daily choices.

Moving beyond mere personal reflection, our insights inspire a call to communal action, urging us to build communities grounded in the tenets of faith and love. They impel us to bridge divides, foster healing, and establish places of sanctuary where Marian principles of compassion and mercy are lived. As individuals, our reflections deepen our devotion; as a collective, these insights transform vision into reality, guiding us toward a hopeful future guided by Marian light.

Ultimately, these reflections bind us to the spiritual heritage of the Church, offering an intimate connection with the divine and an invitation to participate in the rich tradition of Marian devotion. The messages of Medjugorje echo the timeless wisdom that, despite our weaknesses, we are called to a higher purpose, one intertwined with love, justice, and peace. In this sacred dialogue with Mary, we discover insights that inspire action and reflection, deepening our bonds with the divine and urging us towards a fulfillment of heavenly promises.

In embracing this reflective journey, may we find clarity, renewal, and an ever-deepening faith that aligns with the divine intention woven into our very beings. We are pilgrims, wandering through temporal landscapes, yet always reaching towards something infinitely divine, thus transforming ourselves and the world one act of devotion at a time. As the chapters of Medjugorje continue to unfold, so too will our personal insights in this ever-evolving spiritual journey.

Chapter 17: Testimonies of Miracles

In the ethereal landscape of Medjugorje, where the celestial meets the terrestrial, testimonies of miracles ripple through the faithful like echoes of a timeless hymn. Here, the faithful gather, their hearts open like lilies to the sun, ready to receive the grace of the Divine. Stories of miraculous healings, both of the body and the spirit, unfold as chapters of an unwritten gospel, each one echoing the unfathomable love at the heart of the cosmos. Pilgrims speak of maladies that vanish, leaving behind nothing but the sweet fragrance of hope; of hearts once shrouded in despair, bathed anew in the light of peace. In these encounters with the miraculous, the lines between the natural and the supernatural blur, drawing each witness deeper into the sacred narrative, a testament as ancient as the faith that sustains them. As these miracles unfold, they not only stand as beacons of divine intervention but also as profound affirmations of the messages that the seers of Medjugorje share, intertwining the heavenly with the earthly in a quilt of enduring faith and devotion.

Documented Miraculous Events

The town of Medjugorje, nestled in the rugged terrain of Bosnia and Herzegovina, has captured the hearts of many around the globe. Its name echoes in the halls of faith, whispered in the same breath as other hallowed sites that speak of divine intervention. The apparitions at Medjugorje aren't just idle tales; they've generated a profound testimony— vivid stories of miraculous events that demand attention with a blend of awe and reverence.

A lived experience of time-bound miracles begins to unfold when we consider the documented evidence. From the very first whispered mysteries to the present-day declarations, Medjugorje has been a beacon of hope, offering extraordinary phenomena that defy rational explanation. These events, attested by pilgrims and seers alike, paint a picture not only of wonder but of a tangible connection to the divine. Variations in experiences converge in a singular, consistent witness—a reliance on faith that asserts these are truly acts beyond the mundane.

One of the most compelling documented signs involves the sun itself. Numerous reports detail how the sun danced erratically, projecting an aurora of colors that mesmerizes onlookers and leaves them in introspective silence. Witnesses describe how it pulsates, almost like a living entity, exuding warmth without overheating. The phenomenon is said to recur before the eyes of the faithful, creating a shared vision that invites both introspection and celebration.

Among the intricate chronicles of celestial wonders, another recurring event includes the appearance of luminous crosses in the skies over Medjugorje. These celestial markings are said to hover in the azure expanse, etched indignantly against the twilight. Many claim these images serve as divine signatures, assurances of Our Lady's presence and a testament to the sacred revelation through the fabric of this place.

Moreover, the hill of apparitions, a revered site of pilgrimage, envelops numerous testimonies of physical and spiritual healing. Countless pilgrims recount stories of ailments lifted and maladies dissolved, where conventional medicine found itself at a standstill. While science strives to explain away these occurrences as psychological or coincidental, those who have experienced them carry an emotional conviction that defies logical dissection.

Some tales stand out, firmly embedded in the memory of devotees. There are stories of individuals blind from birth receiving sight as they gaze upon the silhouette of the Virgin. These narratives don't merely detail the restoration of physical senses, but speak to a revival of faith and purpose. The newly sighted describe perceiving a world bathed anew in divine light, where every detail is a brushstroke in a divine masterpiece.

The Rosary, an emblematic devotion within Roman Catholicism, finds a miraculous ally in Medjugorje. Witnesses attest to the spontaneous transformation of rosaries from their base metal to a shimmering gold hue. This phenomenon captures the imagination by blending symbolic meaning with tangible evidence, offering spiritual seekers a profound sense of connection and reverence.

Some experiences, too delicate to confine within written texts, speak to the soft whispers of Mary herself. Those who listen with open hearts recount hearing messages of peace and love, transmitted through a voice both soft and serene. These vocal incantations are said to resonate within, strengthening resolve and deepening belief. Such encounters serve as personal affirmations, emblems of the divine that are not presented to jest, but to nurture the soul.

Furthermore, certain events have been recorded with meticulous attention, feeding the appetites of scholars eager to bridge the gap between faith and evidence. Video footage, photographs, and eyewitness accounts become a sprawling archive of the extraordinary. These documentations submit to no impartial scrutiny with a muted elegance, while others claim them to be incontrovertible proof of the transcendent.

Despite the pageantry of celestial acts and physical healings, it's the transformation of lives—the deepest of miracles—that occupies the heart of Medjugorje. Testimonies of conversion, forgiveness, and newfound hope emerge from the shadowy recesses of human suffering. Individuals shackled by addiction and despair testify to liberation through an encounter with a presence that defies human articulation. It is in these personal stories that the sacred dances alongside the miraculous, leaving indelible fingerprints on the soul.

Critics and skeptics may scrutinize these tales, wielding the sword of doubt, but to the countless pilgrims who have felt the ethereal pulse of Medjugorje, these events resonate as unshakeable truths. The construct of miracles at Medjugorje serves as an invitation—a plea for fidelity not only to the extraordinary but to the sanctity of what lies beyond the veil. An invitation that whispers to the spirit and beckons the faithful to delve deeper into the mystery of divine manifestation.

Personal Accounts of Healing and Transformation

In the silent embrace of Medjugorje's rolling hills, an unfathomable mystery has unfurled—a legacy woven with accounts of personal healing and spiritual transformation. Here, amidst the palpable echoes of divine messages, pilgrims have experienced encounters that defy the limitations of earthly understanding. Through the stories shared by souls transformed, the place of Medjugorje transcends its physical borders, becoming a beacon of hope and a cauldron of miracles.

For many, the journey to Medjugorje begins with a heart burdened by despair or a spirit weighed down by the relentless trials of life. Yet, as they tread the well-worn paths, an intangible serenity begins to envelop them. Such was the experience of Anna, who arrived seeking solace from a protracted illness that had stripped her of both health and hope. In the sacrament of confession, within a humble church nestled against a backdrop of towering mountains, she found more than absolution. Leaving that sacred space, she felt a profound release, her ailment inexplicably lightened, as if carried away by the whispering breeze.

Others speak of transformations not of the body, but of the soul, a metanoia—a renewal of faith and purpose. For John, whose spirit had languished in the shadows of grief after the loss of his only son, Medjugorje offered him an encounter with divine mercy. As he knelt in prayerful surrender beneath the towering crucifix on Krizevac Hill, a warmth enveloped his heart. In that moment, the chains of sorrow began to fall away, replaced by a tranquil acceptance and a rekindled spark of hope that seemed to echo the ancient promise of resurrection.

Personal stories from Medjugorje illuminate a spectrum of experiences encompassing the physical, emotional, and spiritual realms. They tell of the gentle intercession of Our Lady, whose presence in visions and messages has been a consoling balm for the disillusioned and the disheartened. Lourdes, a lifelong skeptic, found her skepticism dissolving in the quietude of evening apparitions. In the soft, embracing darkness, she perceived a clarity that was neither visible nor tangible, but unmistakable—a conviction that her life had meaning beyond the mundane struggles and uncertainties. It was as if a veil had been lifted, allowing her to glimpse the divine choreography behind every twist of fate.

For some pilgrims, encounters at Medjugorje have manifested in extraordinary phenomena, bolstering the conviction of the faithful and challenging the incredulity of cynics. There are accounts of rosary beads turning a golden hue, and crucifixes rejecting the weight of earthly corrosion. Such signs, while wondrous, serve a dual purpose—to awaken faith in those who witness them and to remind the affected of the deeper, often unseen, miracles taking place within their hearts.

Through prayer and reflection, these miracles bring about a sharpened awareness, an alignment with Sacred Tradition and Scripture. Here, unassuming individuals discover the profound truth woven through their own narratives, finding their lives entwined with the sacred stories of the past. In the transformative ambiance of Medjugorje, the past and present merge in a living testament to divine grace.

Consider Maria, a young mother from South America, whose heart was engulfed in fear for her children's future amidst a world of uncertainties. Her visit to Medjugorje was punctuated by an experience at Apparition Hill where she claimed to have seen the gentle visage of Our Lady, her face radiant with peace and maternal love. This encounter infused Maria with a previously unfathomable courage, prompting her to pursue personal missions of compassion back home, dedicating herself to orphaned children. Maria's heart was now aflame with a desire to emulate the love she had witnessed, transforming anxiety into action.

For some, the transformation unfolds not as an epiphanous event but as a gradual unfolding of the soul, like a flower opening to the sun's first light. Yet, the cumulative power of these transformations challenges the preconceived limitations of the human heart, hinting at the infinite possibilities of divine intervention. The realizations and awakenings that occur in Medjugorje invite a reexamination of life's ultimate purpose. Parish notices proclaim campaigns of reparation, forgiveness, and renewal, echoing the calls of Our Lady for prayer, penance, and peace.

Countless pilgrims touch upon a newfound zeal for the rosary, weaving its mysteries into their daily lives. The rhythmic cadence of the prayers binds them with an invisible thread to countless generations who have sought refuge in their recitation. In these quiet moments—whether in solitude or joined with others in the humble chapels—they discover a sacred dialogue that transcends the confines of time, drawing them closer to the divine mystery.

It is in Medjugorje's seeming simplicity where profound complexities unravel. Healing and transformation here are not merely about overcoming ailments or resolving crises, but about an intimate encounter with the sacred that calls forth a more authentic and enriched way of being. Here, stories of change do not end with the departure from Medjugorje's embrace. Instead, they echo forward, rippling into the future, influencing choices and bearing witness to the inexhaustible font of divine grace.

These personal accounts, lodged in the memories of those who have walked the paths of Medjugorje, stand as living testaments to the ethereal presence that has called many to return to the heart of faith. The variety of transformations, like stars scattered across a canopy of night, each shines with its own story, yet collectively they illuminate a profound truth—the sacred union of human spirit and divine love is not mere legend but a profound reality for those open to its embrace.

Thus, the narrative of healing and transformation within Medjugorje continues to unfold, a testament to the power of faith and the enduring promise of the miraculous. Each pilgrim carries a bit of Medjugorje within them—a hope, a memory, a mission—each contributing to the fabric of faith as bright threads of divine grace continue to guide and transform lives across the world.

Chapter 18: Pilgrimage Experience

As pilgrims embark on their sacred journey to Medjugorje, they encounter a landscape where the divine seems to palpably touch the mundane, each stone and path echoing hymns of celestial devotion. The anticipation builds as they prepare for this spiritual odyssey, not merely as a voyage of miles but as an inward pilgrimage of the soul. Amidst the serene hills and echoes of fervent prayers, these seekers find themselves enveloped in a narrative replete with the countless testimonies of faith and transformation. Each step along the dusty trails is a step through time and spirit, drawing them closer to the divine. Witnessing the heartfelt devotion of fellow pilgrims, and the profound simplicity of faith that transcends language and culture, one's heart finds itself aligned with the eternal cadence of heaven's call. The pilgrimage becomes a profound witness to the grace and messages bestowed upon this humble village, affirming the heart's deepest longing for peace and divine presence.

Preparing for a Pilgrimage to Medjugorje

A pilgrimage to Medjugorje is not just a journey; it is a profound spiritual adventure that draws the heart closer to the divine mysteries revealed through the Virgin Mary's apparitions. Before setting forth on such a sacred expedition, pilgrims must prepare both physically and spiritually to receive the abundant graces that await them. This preparation is akin to embarking on a transformative quest, where both the mind and soul align with the celestial messages that Medjugorje promises to reveal.

Physical preparation might seem straightforward, involving arranging travel, preparing luggage, and ensuring one is physically able to undertake the journey. Yet it is more than that. Pilgrims should take time to study the landscape and culture of Medjugorje, understanding that this village is a replete with history, faith, and simple living. The terrain itself, which includes Apparition Hill and Cross Mountain, requires physical readiness. Many pilgrims choose to walk these paths barefoot, connecting themselves to the earth and embracing humility. Such acts encourage a sense of lassitude from the material world, urging a focus on simplicity and prayer.

Beyond the physical preparation, one must embark on an inner journey. This spiritual readiness is crucial, and it involves prayer, reflection, and an openness to the divine will. Pilgrims often engage in prayer novenas dedicated to Our Lady of Medjugorje, asking for guidance and blessings. It's a period of eager anticipation, filled with meditations on the messages given by the Blessed Virgin, emphasizing peace, conversion, and faith. These messages echo continuously through one's mind, inviting introspection and a deepening desire for personal transformation.

Moreover, understanding the significance of continuous prayer during this preparation period cannot be overstated. The rosary, an integral part of Medjugorje's spirituality, becomes a lifeline, each bead a stepping stone toward the celestial. Pilgrims are encouraged to pray the rosary daily, entwining their intentions with those of countless others who have traveled this path. This shared spiritual exercise crafts a communal bond, a network of grace that surrounds the pilgrim with divine protection and support.

The essence of fasting also plays a pivotal role in preparing for this pilgrimage. Fasting isn't merely the abstinence from food; it represents the shedding of worldly concerns, a purifying act that strengthens spiritual resolve. Many pilgrims adhere to fasting on bread and water on Wednesdays and Fridays as suggested in Medjugorje's messages. Through fasting, the soul confronts its weaknesses while being fortified, tuning itself to hear the whisperings of the Holy Spirit. In this penitential practice, there's a stripping away of unnecessary burdens, allowing for a more profound encounter with God's love and mercy.

Emotional and mental preparation should not be overlooked. This pilgrimage opens a gateway to the heart, unveiling layers of past grievances, unhealed traumas, and hidden fears. Pilgrims are encouraged to bring these before God, seeking healing and release. Journaling becomes a powerful tool in this journey, where one can document thoughts, prayers, and resolutions. Recording these reflections acts as both a mirror and a window—offering a glimpse into one's spiritual growth and unresolved struggles. Writing inherently encourages an honest dialogue with oneself, facilitating a transformation that aligns one's for the pilgrimage.

An awareness of community dynamics in Medjugorje also informs how one prepares spiritually and emotionally. Pilgrims often travel in groups, creating a microcosm of fellowship akin to the early Christian communities. This communal aspect offers mutual support and shared experiences that underscore the pilgrimage's transformative potential. Discussions, prayer circles, and shared meals build a collective consciousness among pilgrims, further enriching their journey.

As pilgrims prepare, it is crucial to remain open to the unexpected. Medjugorje's beauty is found in its unpredictability, where the divine gently disrupts human plans to unfold something greater. The apparitions speak of a heavenly order and call to sanctity, yet they often arrive in the simplicity of life's moments, teaching and transforming in quiet and profound ways. Thus, expectations should remain fluid, allowing for God's grace to manifest organically.

No true pilgrimage to Medjugorje is complete without a heart ready to receive and a mind attuned to listen. As one embarks upon this sacred journey, it is a time of profound reconnection with God, an opportunity to step away from the cacophony of the world and listen to the whispers of the divine. With each step in Medjugorje, the pilgrim walks not just on earth but strides closer towards a heavenly understanding, where the messages of Medjugorje illuminate the path to sanctity and divine love.

And so, with prayerful preparation and a yearning spirit, the pilgrim moves forward—a seeker of truth, a bearer of hope, stepping into the mystery that is Medjugorje. It stands as a living testament to faith, a reminder that true preparation begins not with the journey to Medjugorje, but within the sacred corridors of the heart.

Personal Accounts and Reflections

Walking the cobbled paths of Medjugorje, a sense of the sacred permeates the air. It's not surprising that pilgrims from all walks of life and corners of the earth find themselves here, searching for connection, meaning, and a brush with the divine. Each journey is as unique as the individual undertaking it, yet there is often a common thread of transformation that weaves through the stories of those who have been touched by this place.

Consider the experience of Maria, a humble woman from Spain. She arrived in Medjugorje with a heart burdened by doubt and grief, seeking solace and clarity. The moment she set foot in the Apparition Hill, as many others have described, she felt enveloped by an inexplicable peace. It wasn't the legendary beauty of the landscape that stirred her spirit but an inner serenity that she hadn't known in years. Maria later recounted that during her time at the hill, she felt compelled to let go of her doubts and to welcome a renewed sense of faith.

Another extraordinary account comes from Thomas, a young scholar with a skeptical mind. His visit to Medjugorje was driven more by curiosity than devotion, yet it became a pivotal chapter in his spiritual journey. Initially, Thomas approached the experience as one might an academic inquiry—analytical and detached. However, as he spent more time absorbing the messages and participating in daily prayers, he found his skepticism unraveling. His transformation was not immediate but gradual, like the unfolding of a flower, bringing him to a deeper understanding of the unity between reason and faith.

It's important to recognize that these revelations are deeply personal and nuanced. Pilgrims like Maria and Thomas experience a profound awakening, shaped not only by their physical presence in Medjugorje but by an internal dialogue spurred by their surroundings. Such experiences are echoed in countless reflections—each providing a testament to the mystery and grace that many find here.

For some, Medjugorje sheds light on a lifelong calling that had been quiet or unrecognized. Take, for example, Anna, who discovered her vocation during a night of adoration at St. James Church. Faced with the flickering candlelight and enveloped in the community of believers praying around her, she discerned a call to a deeper service. It's as if Medjugorje acted as a catalyst, allowing her to hear the whispering of her soul more clearly than ever before.

Similarly, a man named David shares his transformation story. A seasoned journalist well-versed in the pursuit of facts and cynicism, he began writing a documentary piece on Medjugorje with the hopes of uncovering hidden truths. What unfolded instead was a journey of personal realization. The simple, yet profound act of joining a group recitation of the Rosary opened his heart to dimensions of faith he couldn't justify through logic alone.

These accounts highlight a paradox: in Medjugorje, the physical journey often parallels a much deeper spiritual pilgrimage. Pilgrims find themselves undergoing an internal transformation that defies the temporal and material. For all the mystique around the miracles and visions, it's the subtle, intimate interactions with the divine that leave a lasting imprint on each heart.

As these pilgrims reflect on their experiences, they often articulate a sensation that time itself shifts here—each moment feels imbued with eternity. Whether it's in the silence of contemplation or the collective energy of group prayers, Medjugorje invites them into a dance of time where the spiritual becomes tangible and transformative.

This remarkable place holds a mirror to its visitors' hearts, reflecting back their own desires for peace, forgiveness, and unity. It's both a humbling and elevating experience, drawing individuals out of their singular pursuits into a greater communal exchange with others and the divine.

Some pilgrims develop lifelong bonds with individuals they meet during their stay, finding spiritual kinship that transcends language and culture. These relationships often mirror the unity advocated in the messages claimed to be from Our Lady of Medjugorje, encouraging a universal brotherhood anchored in love and forgiveness.

In chronicling the personal accounts of pilgrims like Maria, Thomas, Anna, and David, it is evident that Medjugorje is much more than a destination; it's a heart-altering mission. People arrive expecting modest revelations or perhaps none at all, only to depart with souls rejuvenated and visions clearer—the echoes of which resonate far beyond the borders of Bosnia and Herzegovina.

Finally, standing in reflection at Medjugorje, one can't help but acknowledge a divine orchestration at play. The quiet evidence of transformation, seen through the eyes of swayed visitors, speaks countlessly of the handiwork of the divine upon hearts prepared to receive it. It leaves an indelible mark—a celestial signature on the parchment of human existence.

These narratives and reflections remind us that life's true voyage begins where the tangible world meets the unknown, igniting a luminous path that draws us deeper into the heart of faith, purpose, and love. Medjugorje stands as a testament to that pilgrimage, quietly compelling the faithful and the seeking to embark on their own journey toward transcendence and communal spirituality.

Chapter 19: Criticisms and Controversies

In any spiritual awakening as profound as the Medjugorje apparitions, a whirlwind of criticisms and controversies is almost inevitable. Skeptics question the authenticity of the visions and the divine nature of the messages delivered by the seers, often scrutinizing them against a backdrop of historical precedent and doctrinal orthodoxy. Not all inquiries are born of cynicism, though; some arise from genuine concern for the preservation of faith's integrity within the sacred traditions of the Church. The Vatican's response has been measured, balancing caution with openness, acknowledging the genuine spiritual fruits borne of the Medjugorje phenomenon while maintaining rigorous discernment. The Church seeks not to stifle the flames of faith sprouting in Medjugorje but to ensure that new devotions complement rather than contradict the canon of established teachings. Through the storm of debate, the faithful are challenged to delve deeper, merging reason with faith, to discern the harmonious blend of revelation and tradition. This crucible of contention, therefore, invites a richer, more resilient engagement with the divine, urging believers to reflect on the messages' alignment with both sacred scripture and the lived experience of Catholic devotion.

Addressing Common Criticisms

The subject of Medjugorje draws attention from many corners, raising questions that often stem from the skepticism inherent in facing the divine mysteries. One cannot deny that skepticism has its place; after all, it encourages discernment. But we should also navigate this sea of criticisms with an open heart, seeking the guiding light of faith as much as the evidence we dissect.

A prevailing critique concerns the nature and frequency of the apparitions themselves. Critics often ask how visions lasting so many years align with traditional Catholic belief. They argue that such lengthy apparitions are unprecedented. But we need to consider the unique timing of these experiences. Viewed through the lens of Sacred Tradition, the messages are a clarion call tailored for a world in dire need of spiritual awakening. The unprecedented scope aligns with the unprecedented challenges of our time.

Another common criticism lies in the perceived discrepancies between the seers' messages and established Church doctrine. Skeptics worry about potential contradictions. However, it's essential to acknowledge that private revelations, like those of Medjugorje, don't alter the deposit of faith; they merely shed new light on it. The teachings offered through these visions often serve as a reminder of the core tenets already present in Sacred Scripture and Tradition—peace, prayer, penance, and conversion.

Critics also raise concerns about the economic and commercial aspects of the pilgrimage site, questioning the authenticity of the messages in light of perceived financial motivation. True, the rise of Medjugorje as a pilgrimage destination brings with it the bustle of commerce. Yet, it is essential to recognize that the spiritual transformation reported by countless pilgrims can't be reduced to mere economic equations. The experiences of many reveal profound personal conversions and deepened faith that transcend monetary considerations.

The issue of ecclesiastical approval—or lack thereof—often fuels critics' arguments. They emphasize that the Vatican hasn't given formal recognition to the apparitions. Here, a nuanced understanding is critical. The Church often takes its time in discerning such matters, allowing the fruits to manifest over years, if not decades. While formal approval remains pending, the Church has permitted organized pilgrimages, signaling a recognition of the pilgrimage site's positive spiritual impact.

Some theological critiques focus on comparing Medjugorje's messages to established Marian apparitions. They note different themes and frequencies, questioning whether the deviation signifies falsehood. However, it's crucial to appreciate the diverse ways Mary has historically chosen to communicate. The variance in her messages, from Lourdes to Fatima and Medjugorje, reflects the distinct spiritual needs of each epoch. Variety doesn't imply contradiction; it enriches the construct of Marian devotion.

Skeptics occasionally question the backgrounds and motivations of the seers themselves, suggesting potential manipulation. Yet, the enduring faith and humility exhibited by these individuals over the decades counter such allegations. Their lives have been scrutinized, yet their consistent witness to the messages' spiritual depth showcases a credibility that withstands the test of time.

One more criticism demands attention: the supposed lack of miraculous evidence. While critics may expect overt signs and wonders, the true miracle often lies in subtler forms—in transformed lives and hearts renewed by grace. The ripple effect of conversion stories, peace-building efforts, and heightened Marian devotion among pilgrims constitutes an everyday miracle that often escapes the cynic's gaze.

While examining these criticisms, we shouldn't overlook the role that faith itself plays in understanding these mysteries. Faith, after all, operates in a realm beyond empirical measurement. Critics can scrutinize historical accuracy, theological soundness, and economic implications, but they may struggle to fathom the spiritual nourishment the messages provide. This nourishment manifests in the peace, hope, and renewal found by countless individuals who engage sincerely with the Medjugorje phenomenon.

In conclusion, the criticisms and questions surrounding the Medjugorje apparitions challenge believers to a deeper discernment—a call to engage with the messages and their implications thoughtfully. By aligning these messages with Sacred Tradition and Scripture, by focusing on spiritual fruits over sensational signs, and by trusting in the time-tested process of Church discernment, we invite a balanced perspective. Criticism need not diminish faith; instead, it can refine it, urging us towards a more profound understanding of divine action in our world.

Let us, then, embrace these criticisms not as obstacles, but as stepping stones that guide us closer to the truth. In doing so, we follow the path of many saints who transformed skepticism into deeper devotion, welcoming challenges as opportunities for grace. This journey, though fraught with questions, beckons us toward the light of Medjugorje's message—a call to prayer, peace, and unwavering faith.

Church Response to Controversies

The swirling controversies surrounding the apparitions at Medjugorje have evoked a variety of responses from within the Church. Generally, the Church approaches such matters with a prudence that reflects her millennia of discernment and wisdom. In understanding the Church's response, it's essential to separate the genuine spiritual fruits from any confusion or misinformation that may arise.

Historically, the Church adopts a cautious and methodical stance when evaluating private revelations, and Medjugorje is no exception. The process of approval or disapproval is normally conducted through a series of investigations to verify the supernatural nature of any claimed apparition. The diocesan bishop is usually the primary authority in the early stages of evaluation, reviewing testimonies, reported miracles, and other relevant phenomena.

In the case of Medjugorje, various commissions have been established to study the events. While these investigations were ongoing, the Church maintained a neutral stance, neither fully endorsing nor condemning the apparitions. This has allowed space for continued pilgrimages and personal devotion while ensuring that the faithful are not misled into false belief or devotion that is not in line with Church teaching.

The Church recognizes the distinction between divine revelations, which ended with the death of the last apostle, and private revelations, which are personal messages believed to come from God or saints, intended for the guidance of individuals or communities. Thus, the Church exercises careful discernment to determine whether a private revelation, like those claimed at Medjugorje, aligns with biblical and traditional teachings.

In 2010, the Vatican established a commission led by Cardinal Camillo Ruini to conduct a more thorough investigation into the Medjugorje events. This commission was tasked with examining the spiritual and pastoral issues surrounding the apparitions. Its findings, submitted to the Congregation for the Doctrine of the Faith, offered a comprehensive perspective on how the Church should address the claims and controversies of Medjugorje.

Overall, the Church's response to Medjugorje reflects a careful balance of claims and evidence. It embodies a recognition of the spiritual fruit that has emerged from the site, evidenced by conversions, vocations, and personal transformations experienced by thousands of pilgrims. Personal testimonies of deepened faith and miraculous events are cautiously acknowledged while maintaining doctrinal integrity.

Pope Francis himself has spoken about Medjugorje, underlining the importance of ensuring that any devotion stemming from it leads the faithful closer to God and conforms to the teachings of the Church. He emphasizes that the reported Marian apparitions should be approached with openness to the Holy Spirit while maintaining the prudence and guidance of Church doctrine.

The role of tradition and scripture in evaluating Medjugorje is pivotal. The Church defends its tradition as a lens through which private revelations should be tested. Consequently, any message or apparition must not contradict Sacred Tradition and Sacred Scripture. This is not just a matter of safeguarding doctrine but ensuring that the faithful's journey remains aligned with the path to holiness revealed through Jesus Christ.

The Church also concerns itself with potential misunderstandings that can arise with private revelations. Misinterpretation or sensationalism can cloud the true fruits of a professed apparition. Therefore, pastoral guidance has been emphasized to aid believers in understanding the value of the messages proclaimed at Medjugorje within the broader context of the Catholic faith.

In addressing controversies, the Church uses her wisdom and authority to avoid rash judgments, recognizing that premature conclusions can harm both individuals' faith journeys and the broader Catholic community. It's critical to the Church's mission to foster environments where truth, faith, and a deep devotion to God flourish.

Medjugorje continues to be a beacon for many, symbolizing a call to prayer, conversion, and new hope. Through a cautious yet open-minded approach, the Church aims to discern the authenticity of these apparitions while actively engaging in the spiritual welfare of the faithful. It is within this tranquil embrace of both skepticism and belief that Medjugorje remains a subject of profound intrigue and spiritual exploration within the Church.

Chapter 20: The Future of Medjugorje

As we stand on the brink of what lies ahead for Medjugorje, we find ourselves in a landscape woven with both divine mystery and tangible hope. The visions have not only echoed through the hearts of pilgrims, but they have also kindled a fire of faith that burns bright in the modern Church. While we venture forward, we are beckoned by Our Lady's celestial summons, which calls for a steadfast commitment to the messages of peace, prayer, and conversion as handed down through Sacred Tradition and illuminated by Sacred Scripture. The future of Medjugorje is not merely an unfolding narrative but a living testament that seeks to transform the echo of the seers into a symphony of collective devotion. With each new dawn, the legacy continues, beckoning believers to heed this sacred call and to fortify the bonds of community through shared prayer and love. In this unity, we find the luminous pathway that will guide the faithful towards holiness and eternal peace, while encouraging a pervasive transformation that extends beyond borders and hearts, lighting the way for generations to come.

Predictions and Expectations

The future of Medjugorje, is a subject of boundless intrigue and anticipation. Within the whispers of the hills and the sacred echo of Our Lady's messages, lies a journey that beckons believers and skeptics alike. What does the destiny of Medjugorje hold? While definitive answers remain cloaked in mystery, we can speculate, informed by the rich tradition of Marian apparitions and guided by the messages imparted to the seers.

First, one might imagine a deepening global recognition of Medjugorje as a beacon of faith and spiritual renewal. The apparition site already stands as a testament to the thirst for divine connection in an ever-disconnected world, drawing millions to its sacred grounds. As time unfolds, expect a continued influx of pilgrims, seekers whose own spiritual quests are invigorated by the palpable sense of holiness that envelops Medjugorje.

If history rhymes with the divine narrative present in other Marian apparitions, Medjugorje could very well mirror the paths of Fatima and Lourdes, integrating itself deeper within the universal consciousness of the faithful. This would not only fortify its standing within the Catholic Church but also offer a universal call to unity, promoting peace and reconciliation across diverse beliefs. The apparition site could serve as a spiritual crossroads, inviting dialogue and understanding.

Some theologians and biblical scholars predict that the messages of Medjugorje will continue to influence and inspire the evolving dynamics within the Church. The Church, led by the Holy Spirit, may find itself more open to acknowledging the voice of the faithful and the significance of private revelations as a spiritual supplement to the eternal truths cherished within Catholicism. This openness could inspire deeper contemplation on ecclesiastical structures, reinforcing a call to sanctity and reflection on the ecclesial mission in today's world.

Economic and social factors cannot be discounted when considering Medjugorje's future. The town's transformation into a hub of pilgrimage offers opportunities and challenges alike. With increased attention comes the potential for economic growth, yet balance must be struck to preserve the sacredness of this site. One might expect the local community and Church authorities to collaborate closely, ensuring that the simple message of Our Lady is not overwhelmed by commercial interests.

The messages given to the seers have often alluded to future events and circumstances, laden with calls for conversion, prayer, and peace. While specifics may remain unrevealed, these directives can be interpreted as timeless, providing a roadmap not just for individuals, but for societies navigating turbulent waters. Central to these messages is the notion of personal transformation—a perennial expectation that faith enacted through prayer and penance can usher in an era of prevailing peace.

Considering the temporal and eternal dimensions of Medjugorje's messages, there arises a question of how they might be manifested in global affairs. Can Medjugorje influence geopolitical currents, sway hearts from a path of division to one of unity? While such assertions might seem grandiose, the seen and unseen power of faith, aligned with divine will, has historically catalyzed profound change. The future could witness Medjugorje as a catalyst for peace, echoing Mary's perpetual intercession for humanity.

Moreover, as society grapples with moral and spiritual crises, there's an expectation that Medjugorje will offer steadfast guidance. Its messages may grow ever more relevant in the face of modern challenges: from technological advancements that reshape human interaction to existential questions around identity and purpose. These messages, steeped in spiritual wisdom, remind us of the necessity to keep prayer and reflection alive amid noise and distraction.

As with any prophetic vision, room must be made for divine surprise. Predictions about Medjugorje must remain open to the mysteries of faith, cognizant that the ways of God don't always align with human expectations or timelines. The role of Medjugorje in the future might defy conventional reasoning yet fulfill a higher promise only discernible through faith and devoted expectation.

Finally, what about the legacy Medjugorje might offer future generations? The hope is for a lineage unbroken by time, continuing to inspire through its testimony of love, peace, and redemption. As successive generations uncover the messages anew, they stand poised to draw transformative insights, propelling them towards a more profound unity with the divine.

The journey ahead for Medjugorje resonates with a sacred promise—a celestial call to live in alignment with eternal truths. Whether simple or profound, these predictions nurture a hopeful expectation, inviting all to listen to the whispers of the divine, poised on the brink of an unforeseen grace.

Continuing the Legacy

The story of Medjugorje isn't confined to its past or the present moment; it stretches into the future, with tendrils of hope and spirituality touching lives worldwide. As we consider the legacy it leaves, we must ponder how it continues to inspire faith and devotion in a rapidly changing world. The apparitions and messages challenge us to uphold a spiritual tradition while encouraging personal transformation.

Central to this legacy is the unwavering commitment to peace that has resonated in the hearts of those who have listened carefully. The call to arms isn't with weapons but with rosaries and prayers, as the Medjugorje messages beckon us towards a world where serenity reigns. In a time when discord and division threaten to unravel the fabric of society, the enduring message of Medjugorje serves as a beacon of hope, inspiring believers to strive for harmony in their personal and communal lives.

Furthermore, the legacy of Medjugorje is laden with an invitation to a life of prayer and sacrifice. The seers have consistently conveyed messages emphasizing prayer as a path to spiritual renewal and fasting as a means to embrace humility and empathy. In adhering to these practices, the faithful are called not just to observe, but to embody a lifestyle that reflects divine intercession at Medjugorje. This resonance of tradition with daily practice strengthens the belief that heaven's messages have a tangible place in everyday life.

The conversations sparked by Medjugorje's messages also forge a deeper, more profound alignment with Holy Scripture and Tradition. It evokes a feeling akin to rediscovering an ancient relic buried within one's own heart—the convergence of these messages with the timeless teachings of the Church reaffirms their sacred origin. This alignment not only authenticates the revelations but invites us to explore the profound truths enshrined in both Scripture and personal experience.

The worldwide pilgrimage to Medjugorje embarks from a thirst for connection to something greater than ourselves. For many, a journey to this sacred place signifies more than physically visiting a distant land; it invites a profound inward journey, often culminating in a sense of peace and clarity—gifts of the heart's true pilgrimage. While modern pilgrims venture to Medjugorje seeking these gifts, they, in turn, become ambassadors, carrying the seeds of their spiritual experiences back to their communities, and thus, continuing the living legacy of Medjugorje.

The testimonies of miracles and conversions abound, adding layers to the legacy Medjugorje leaves. These accounts weave together a fabric of divine interaction, painting a vivid picture of transformation and faith renewal. The stories, varied in detail yet unified in purpose, stir a sense of the miraculous in daily life, inviting skeptics and believers alike to ponder the mysteries of faith. Through these narratives, Medjugorje remains a lively testament to the impact of divine grace on human lives.

Amidst the legacy's expansion, challenges are inevitable. Criticisms and misunderstandings have arisen, providing impetus for deeper dialogue and reflection. The church's measured and cautious approach to these revelations reflects its role as custodian of truth, ensuring that the phenomena align with the fundamentals of faith. Such scrutiny not only preserves the integrity of the messages but also invites a continued exploration into the nature of divine communication.

A legacy is not merely something we inherit; it's something we're called to cultivate and expand. Those touched by the spirit of Medjugorje are tasked with being its guardians and its voice. By sharing the messages, living the principles, and fostering communities rooted in peace and devotion, the legacy is not just remembered—it becomes actively engaged with the challenges and hopes of each generation.

In envisioning the next chapter of Medjugorje's legacy, we see a future enriched by a deeper understanding of Marian devotion. As more individuals reflect on and commit to the messages, these personal transformations coalesce into a collective spiritual awakening. The legacy of Medjugorje has the potential to nourish the soul of the Church itself, creating rippling effects throughout the lives of the faithful and the structure of Catholicism

The art and culture shaped by Medjugorje's influence further testify to the profound impact of its legacy. Through creative expressions that capture the essence of the apparitions and messages, the story of Medjugorje transcends words and takes visual, musical, and literary form. Each artistic interpretation not only preserves its spiritual essence but also reveals new insights, resonating with those who experience them and inviting continuous dialogue with the divine.

As years unfurl, Medjugorje remains etched in the heart of Christianity, its legacy a is a cacophony of faith, peace, and transformation. The future awaits the echo of the voices who've heard the call and responded with a willingness to engage with the profound mysteries revealed in this small, blessed village. Through each prayer uttered, each pilgrimage made, and every life transformed, we see the continuation of a legacy that forever points towards a deeper communion with heaven.

Chapter 21: Medjugorje and the Modern Church

Amidst the pulsating rhythms of contemporary faith, Medjugorje stands as a beacon, subtly weaving its messages into the fabric of modern Catholicism. This sacred place, echoing with tales of heavenly whispers, challenges the faithful to mold its insights into an evolving Church. Its essence transcends geographical boundaries, inviting a global Catholic community to rethink and reaffirm their spiritual journey. The apparitions at Medjugorje call the modern Church to a renewed commitment, not just in belief, but in action, urging believers to discern the presence of sacred tradition in a world frequently caught in the clamor of secularism. As these celestial encounters intertwine with today's theological dialogues, they kindle a transformative hope, suggesting that the messages of Medjugorje aren't relics of the past but vital instruments of today's spiritual awakening.

The Impact on Global Catholicism

In a world where modernity and tradition often clash, Medjugorje emerges as a beacon of reconciliation and renewal within the Catholic faith. The apparitions that began in the small Bosnian village in 1981 have had profound, rippling effects across the global Catholic community. These apparitions carry a universal message that transcends cultural and geographical borders, uniting believers in a shared spiritual journey.

Medjugorje's impact is not limited to the personal transformations of those who have visited. It has invigorated parishes and religious communities worldwide. Many churches have adopted the Medjugorje emphasis on prayer, fasting, and the Rosary, reviving practices that have waned in contemporary Catholicism. This renewal is not a mere return to the past but a dynamic reintegration of tradition in ways that speak to today's believers.

Beyond practices, the messages from Medjugorje have inspired theological discussion and debate, prompting Catholic scholars to ponder their implications within the framework of existing Church doctrine. In a world where faith can sometimes feel detached from daily life, these reflections encourage believers to see Marian apparitions not as isolated events, but as ongoing callings to a deeper relationship with God.

Medjugorje has also served as a catalyst for ecumenical dialogue. By emphasizing the core values of peace, love, and conversion, the messages have found resonance beyond Catholicism, inviting dialogue between different Christian communities and other faith traditions. This spirit of openness reflects the universal nature of its messages and has enhanced the Church's role as a peacemaker in a fractured world.

The openness of the Vatican and various church authorities to investigate and discuss Medjugorje suggests its significant place in the modern Church. It challenges the faithful to approach apparitions with both discernment and openness. This balance highlights the Church's willingness to evolve while respecting tradition, epitomizing its universal nature — semper reformanda, always reforming.

An often overlooked, yet pivotal aspect of Medjugorje's global impact is its role in the lives of the youth. At Medjugorje, a robust youth movement has flourished, where the messages of peace and conversion cater to young people searching for a sincere and meaningful connection with their faith. Events like the Youth Festival serve as international gatherings where young believers find community and purpose, ushering in a new generation of committed Catholics.

Interestingly, the emphasis on peace and simplicity in Medjugorje resonates strongly with Pope Francis's vision for the Church. This confluence supports a church that emphasizes mercy, humility, and social justice. Medjugorje's messages echo papal calls for simplicity and poverty of spirit, fostering a church more focused on core Gospel values than institutional prestige.

The challenge of Medjugorje extends into realms of evangelization. The worldwide curiosity triggered by Medjugorje presents a unique opportunity to spread the Gospel message to those who might otherwise remain untouched by traditional evangelization efforts. By focusing on personal testimony and conversion, Medjugorje inspires fresh approaches to outreach, especially in multicultural contexts.

Finally, Medjugorje's messages raise profound questions about the nature of the modern Church, particularly concerning technology and communication. As messages once delivered in the quiet of a rural village spread instantly across the globe, they invite reflection on how faith is communicated in a digital age. The challenge is to heed these messages amidst the noise, to find stillness that allows genuine encounter with the divine.

In sum, the apparitions at Medjugorje offer more than spiritual renewal; they challenge the Catholic Church to reassess its role in an interconnected, yet deeply divided world. Whether through fostering shared liturgical practices, inspiring ecumenical conversations, or invigorating youth with a renewed sense of purpose, Medjugorje stands as a remarkable testament to the ongoing and dynamic nature of faith. As the Church continues to engage with these messages, its responses will not only shape the future of Catholicism but also cement Medjugorje's place in its transformative journey.

Medjugorje's Place in Contemporary Faith

In a world that constantly evolves, the place of Medjugorje within contemporary faith offers a profound anchor. This small village has become a lighthouse of spiritual guidance for many who seek deeper connections to their faith. Amid the cacophony of modern life, Medjugorje acts as a gentle provocation, stirring souls to reevaluate their spiritual priorities. It's a place where the divine whispers are heard clearly, urging humanity towards a renewal of faith that aligns with the core tenets of Catholicism.

Medjugorje's significance today can't be overstated. Against the backdrop of secular advances and moral ambiguities, this place serves as a potent reminder of the enduring and unchanging truths found in Sacred Tradition and Sacred Scripture. The apparitions and their messages resonate deeply within the heart of contemporary believers, offering a roadmap to navigate the complexities of modern existence. Like a sacred quilt woven through time, these divine encounters invite believers to weave their own faith journeys into the broader story of redemption.

The Medjugorje phenomenon is a witness to the Church's living, breathing tradition of faith that persists despite centuries of change. It invites contemporary followers to return to the core practices of prayer, penance, and fasting, reinforcing the ancient rhythm of Christian life. These practices, though timeless, have been cast in a new light through the lens of Medjugorje, reminding us that deep spirituality thrives amid simplicity and authenticity. This alignment with tradition not only fortifies individual faith but also strengthens the fabric of community life within the Church.

Furthermore, the messages from Medjugorje speak to a universal desire for peace and reconciliation in a world fractured by discord. They echo a divine urgency to foster a culture of peace that can shape global consciousness. The calls to personal and collective transformation are as relevant today as they were at the beginning of the apparitions. These messages, though nestled in the specifics of one village, reach out beyond borders and cultures, creating a vast spiritual mosaic that encompasses believers from all walks of life.

Engaging with the messages of Medjugorje within the context of contemporary faith demands a willingness to see beyond the limitations of the present. It requires an openness to the transformative power of grace and an understanding that the spiritual journey is both intensely personal and profoundly communal. Medjugorje calls us to be pilgrims in our own right, setting our sights on eternal truths while navigating the transient realities of modern society.

Some might question the relevance of centuries-old traditions in an age marked by rapid change, but Medjugorje stands as a testament to the staying power of genuine faith and divine intervention. Its messages cut through the noise, offering clarity to those willing to listen. The apparitions remind us that, in all our human striving, the greatest truth is found not in innovation but in love, humility, and devotion.

The Church itself reflects on Medjugorje as a living dialogue between heaven and earth. Pilgrims drawn to this holy site are part of a wider ecclesial movement that revitalizes parishes and reinvigorates dioceses worldwide. From personal conversions to widespread communal renewal, Medjugorje intertwines individual encounters with a larger ecclesiastical framework, showcasing the Church's potential to thrive in modernity.

By anchoring ourselves in the messages of Medjugorje, believers find not just a temporary solace, but a lasting transformation that propels them forward with renewed vigor and hope. It's not merely about experiencing the miraculous; it's about allowing these divine encounters to reshape our hearts and actions in service of the Gospel.

In conclusion, Medjugorje holds a pivotal place in contemporary faith as a beacon that calls us back to the essence of our beliefs. Its messages continue to guide, challenge, and encourage the faithful, reinforcing the truth that, at the heart of the modern Church, lies a timeless faith open to the movements of the Spirit. Medjugorje invites all to live fully, love deeply, and trust eternally in God's plan for the world through the lens of its heavenly messages.

Chapter 22: Sharing the Message

In the great apparition and history of Medjugorje's revelations, the chapter titled "Sharing the Message" emerges as a beacon, calling us to play our part in the divine narrative. As pilgrims and stewards of these celestial whispers, we are invited to engage in the joyous task of evangelization, drawing inspiration from the seers' profound experiences. The heavenly messages entrusted to them call for a system of connection, ripe with opportunities to build community imbued with love and understanding. Within this framework, each echo of heaven, like a verse from a sacred hymn, beckons to be shared beyond the bounds of our own hearts. This call to action doesn't merely require a dissemination of words but a living testament of the peace and transformational grace they carry, echoing through our actions and intentions as they knit individuals into a communion of faith. In embracing this commission, we align ourselves with the scriptural mandate to spread the gospel, not as mere heralds, but as living epistles; thus, the messages of Medjugorje become not only a personal revelation but also a shared sacrament that seeds the world with hope, drawing one soul to another in an ever-widening circle of divine love.

Evangelization Through Medjugorje

The hills of Medjugorje rise not just as geographic markers but as spiritual beacons, calling believers and seekers alike to a higher purpose and understanding. Evoking an ancient and profound mystery, the visions and messages emanating from this small Bosnian village reverberate with divine urgency and serene grace. As the sun casts golden hues over the quiet landscape, it illuminates a path toward the heart of evangelization—a path that beckons all who choose to engage with its transformative depths.

In contemplating these august messages, one cannot overlook the instrumental role they play in the symphony of evangelization. Medjugorje serves as a bridge between the celestial and the terrestrial, inviting each soul to participate in a shared journey of faith and devotion. The apparitional messages delivered by the Blessed Virgin Mary here echo the timeless calls of Sacred Tradition and Sacred Scripture, encapsulating central themes such as peace, prayer, and conversion. Through them, believers find both solace and challenge—a gentle, guiding nudge toward evangelizing not only their own spirits but the wider world.

Evangelization, at its core, is about bearing witness to truth. Those touched by the grace of Medjugorje's revelations are called to become bearers of this divine light, living testimonies of miracles that transcend mere human understanding. The seers, with their humble backgrounds and extraordinary encounters, provide a living testament to the authenticity and divine origin of the messages. Their lives are not cloaked in grandeur but are woven into the everyday fabric of believers, illustrating that profound spiritual truth can, and does, reside in simplicity.

The heart of Medjugorje's evangelic power lies in its universality. This universality doesn't dilute its Catholic essence but instead enriches it, allowing a symphony of voices—from different languages, cultures, and backgrounds—to harmonize in shared devotion. The messages, though born in a specific time and space, carry an eternal quality that transcends temporal and geographical boundaries. They resonate as clearly in the bustling city street as they do on a quiet hillside, inviting all to listen, reflect, and act.

Moreover, Medjugorje stands as a testament to the living Church in action. Within its messages rests a powerful call: to renew our hearts, to align them closer with the ultimate truth of the Gospel, and to become instruments of divine love in a fractured world. Such a call to evangelization is not passive. It demands active, lived participation, urging believers to infuse their lives—and, by extension, the lives of those around them—with the essence of the Christ-centered love that the messages advocate.

This evangelistic call reaches its zenith through the community of pilgrims who make their way to this sacred location. Each pilgrim, carrying their own burdens and hopes, becomes part of a broader construct of faith upon encountering the profound peace and spiritual renewal that Medjugorje offers. In sharing personal testimonies and experiences, pilgrims play a crucial role in the ripple effect of evangelization, each story contributing to the larger narrative of God's loving intervention in human history. Through these testimonies, others are invited to explore and perhaps join in this spiritual journey—a journey marked not by destination, but by profound personal transformation.

The Medjugorje messages offer practical guidance, yet they also challenge. They urge believers to immerse themselves in daily practices of prayer and fasting, to deepen their faith through commitment and discernment. In scrutinizing these directives, one uncovers an implicit call to become active evangelizers, to weave these practices into the very fabric of one's daily life. As believers strive to embody these teachings, they become living Gospels, reflecting and spreading the light of Christ in every interaction.

Thus, **the act of evangelizing is inseparably linked to personal conversion and renewal**. As hearts are touched and transformed by the love and instruction offered in Medjugorje, there arises a natural outward flow—a dynamic movement toward sharing this radical encounter with others. It is a journey of passion and perseverance, one imbued with the inevitable trials and moments of doubt but countered by divine grace and strength found in community and prayer.

In essence, evangelization through Medjugorje is more than a call to theological discourse; it is an invitation to live a life authentically informed by divine love and truth. It challenges believers to build communities rooted in faith, to nurture connection through shared spiritual experiences and dialogue, and to embrace diversity within the unity of purpose that Medjugorje espouses. Through this commitment, the legacy of Medjugorje continues, thriving within the hearts of those who dare to share its revolutionary message of hope, peace, and love.

As the sunlight fades over the horizon of this blessed land, one can only marvel at the divine orchestration inherent in Medjugorje's ongoing narrative—a narrative that sustains and rejuvenates the Church of today. This place of encounter, nestled in simplicity and prayer, remains a living testament and beacon to the unending journey of evangelization, ever inviting hearts to awaken to the divine and share the message entrusted to us all.

Building Community and Connection

The notion of community within the context of Medjugorje is essential for spreading the messages entrusted to the seers. These messages, steeped in spiritual richness, are not meant to be kept in isolation but rather to be shared, experienced, and celebrated within a wider communal embrace. In sharing them, an invisible yet formidable system—a network of individuals united by faith, hope, and a shared mission to bring about peace and conversion in the world. Just as the early Christian communities gathered to break bread and share their faith stories, so too the pilgrims and believers tethered to Medjugorje find solace and strength in communal gatherings.

The heart of any thriving community is its capacity to connect individuals on deeper levels than mere acquaintance permits. In Medjugorje, the messages conveyed by the Virgin Mary call each person not only to individual conversion but also to serve as a catalyst for others' spiritual journeys. These gatherings are not just about sharing messages but about living them, allowing them to transform familial, parish, and societal dynamics.

In many ways, these communities mirror the ecclesial movements that punctuate the broader history of the Church. They embody the unity and diversity that characterize the Body of Christ, wherein each member plays a unique role in manifesting the Kingdom of Heaven on Earth. By insofar becoming catalysts of theological reflection and social engagement, Medjugorje communities offer real-world embodiments of divine inspiration.

Community, at its purest, is an echo of the divine relationships within the Holy Trinity. It calls believers to model their interactions on this divine communion, fostering relationships grounded in sacrificial love. Medjugorje communities often see this manifested in acts of charity, communal prayer, and shared rituals. The collective recitation of the Rosary or participation in Eucharistic adoration fortifies bonds, allowing individuals to experience a palpable sense of Oneness with God and their fellow believers.

Moreover, the Medjugorje gatherings serve as fertile ground for spiritual mentorship. Often, individuals who have long nurtured their faith become mentors for newer pilgrims, sharing their insights and experiences to guide others in their spiritual walk. This mentorship echoes Christ's call to make disciples of all nations, offering a tangible way to manifest these heavenly messages. It builds a legacy, teaching newer generations how to integrate these messages into daily life both intuitively and intentionally.

The role of storytelling cannot be overlooked in building this community. Pilgrims share testimonies of conversion, healing, and encounters with the divine that ignite the faith of others. These stories, personal and often miraculous, serve as both encouragement and evidence that the messages are alive and transforming hearts and minds everywhere. The act of sharing stories is inherently connective, creating a narrative thread that binds believers together across geographies and cultures.

In today's digital age, the community and connections inspired by Medjugorje transcend physical boundaries through online platforms and social media. These virtual communities aren't mere shadows of their physical companions; often, they breathe new life into the messages, enabling them to reach corners of the world otherwise inaccessible. Via live-streamed prayer sessions, digital discussions, and message-sharing applications, the impact of Medjugorje extends into the daily scrolls of countless individuals, deeply integrating into the rhythm of modern life.

Furthermore, in the ethos of Medjugorje lies a call for ecumenism. Through its messages of peace and unity, it encourages crossings of denominational lines to form inclusive spiritual networks. These communities provide spaces for dialogues that foster understanding and respect among differing Christian traditions. By focusing on what unites rather than divides, Medjugorje becomes a conduit for building bridges rather than barriers.

Coupled with this inclusive spirit is the call to social action. Inspired by the messages, many communities move beyond theology into praxis. Feeding the hungry, clothing the destitute, advocating for peace, and working for justice mirror the Gospel imperatives while giving flesh to the apparitions' teachings. In these endeavors, the messages of Medjugorje become not only spiritual guideposts but also catalysts for transformative social change.

Ultimately, the community and connections born out of Medjugorje represent a microcosm of the Church's mission in the world. They provide a glimpse into what the Kingdom of God could resemble—a harmonious family united in love and purpose, dedicated to living and spreading the rejuvenating message of peace, conversion, and reconciliation. This divine intent is untangled one strand at a time, yet in its final form, it reveals a breathtaking vision of hope and eternal promise, bringing heaven a little closer to the earth. Through faith and connection, Medjugorje not only revitalizes individual hearts but also invigorates the communal spirit that propels the Church's mission forward.

Chapter 23: Writing Original Medjugorje Reflections

In the sacred embrace of Medjugorje's unfolding mystery, one encounters a spiritual oasis where heaven whispers to the heart's deepest longings. Crafting reflections inspired by these divine apparitions invites one to transcend the mundane, honoring the celestial dialogue that bridges human frailty and divine grace. The art of writing such reflections is akin to painting with words that capture both the ephemeral and the eternal; it merges the fervor of mysticism with the clarity of theological insight. Here, where Marian grace intertwines with the echoes of Sacred Tradition, the writer becomes a conduit for heavenly truths, reflecting the profound simplicity and depth found in the messages bestowed. Each word, chosen with care and reverence, acts as a vessel of transformation, inviting readers to grapple with the perennial call to holiness embedded within the messages of peace, conversion, and divine love. To write of Medjugorje is to echo its spiritual symphony—a harmonious blend of narrative, symbol, and prayer that beckons each soul toward a deeper union with the divine.

Techniques for Writing Spiritually-Inspired Reflections

In the realm of spiritually-inspired reflections, words transform into sacred vessels, carrying whispers of the divine to the soul. As we embark on the task of writing reflections rooted in the ethereal experiences of Medjugorje, it becomes essential for us to listen fervently to these whispers and to convey their richness and depth with sincerity and reverence.

Embarking on this creative endeavor begins with profound immersion into the fabric of Medjugorje's mystical messages and occurrences. To write authentically, one must steep themselves in the details of the visions, the heartfelt messages, and the overwhelming aura of peace and faith that surrounds these events. Only by understanding the spiritual heartbeat of Medjugorje can one authentically reproduce it on paper, resonating with the hearts of the faithful.

One effective technique for crafting such reflections involves prayerful meditation. Before you put pen to paper, spend time in contemplative silence, engaging in dialogue with the divine. Allow the heart and mind to open as vessels to truth, and let this openness guide your thought process and inspire your words. Meditation becomes both a tool and a guide, grounding reflections in a spiritual earnestness that transcends mere literary form.

The use of allegory is invaluable in capturing the essence of Medjugorje's messages. Allegories transform complex spiritual concepts into relatable narratives, making the ethereal tangible. This method allows for deeper connection as it takes abstract divine truths and frames them within the textures of everyday experience. Through allegory, a reflection not only informs but also transforms, making the heavenly not just known, but felt.

Moreover, writing about Medjugorje calls for a poetic sensibility, akin to that found in the Psalms, where the rhythm and resonance of language serve as a conduit for divine grace. Harnessing poetic devices such as metaphor, imagery, and cadence can enrich the spiritual texture of reflections, awakening the reader's soul to the beauty and depth of divine interaction. Through rhythmic prose and vivid descriptions, the sacred comes alive, whispering truths into the heart's ears.

Equally crucial is the infusion of personal narrative within these reflections. Personal experiences and testimonies provide authenticity and relatability, allowing readers to witness the transformative power of Medjugorje through lived experience. This technique invites a personal encounter with the divine, encouraging readers to see parts of their own journey mirrored in the stories shared. Such connection anchors lofty theological concepts in the reality of human experience.

When approaching the task of reflection, it is imperative to engage with Sacred Scripture and Tradition as vital sources of inspiration. Drawing parallels between the messages of Medjugorje and biblical narratives or Church teachings will ground these reflections in a robust theological context, reinforcing their spiritual significance. By rooting reflections in these sacred texts, you offer a faith-led interpretation that aligns personal understanding with the broader system of Christian belief.

The tone adopted in spiritually-inspired writings should echo the serenity and peace found at Medjugorje itself. The language used needs to be both approachable and profound, balancing simplicity with depth. In achieving this, employing a conversational tone can be beneficial, providing a gentle guide through complex spiritual ideas while fostering an intimate dialogue with the reader.

Another vital technique is the integration of questions within the narrative, provoking introspection and deeper engagement. Questions encourage readers to pause and consider, transforming passive reading into active reflection. This method invites readers into a personal dialogue with the text, where they become co-creators of meaning and understanding, guided by the gentle hand of divine invitation.

When writing reflections that are spiritually-inspired, it is also imperative to leave room for mystery. The divine often reveals itself in glimpses and whispers rather than in clarity. To embrace this, writers should allow for ambiguity and wonder, encouraging the reader to dive into the depths of their own spiritual exploration. By doing so, the reflection becomes a journey, not just a destination.

Ultimately, to write reflections inspired by Medjugorje, one should strive to embody the spiritual virtues these events call us to embrace: humility, openness, and love. By approaching the task with a heart set on service and a mind open to divine guidance, reflections will naturally resonate with the spiritual truths they seek to convey. Remembering that writing is not merely a task, but a vocation, infuses these reflections with purpose and power.

Whether you are a seasoned theologian or a budding spiritual seeker, these techniques offer a path to expressing the profound and transformative impact of Medjugorje. With each word, we partake in sharing a celestial melody, contributing to the symphony of faith that has long inspired and uplifted humanity throughout the ages.

Sample Reflections for Personal Use

In the serene embrace of Medjugorje, where the whispers of heaven meet the yearnings of the faithful, we find a rich revelation of spiritual reflections. Each message, each vision, offers a profound opportunity to draw closer to the divine mystery that unfolds amidst the hills of this blessed village. As we embark on our journey to write original reflections inspired by Medjugorje, it becomes imperative to delve deep into our own spiritual experiences, aligning them with the sacred revelations received by the seers. This process, much like the weaving of a fine quilt, requires patience, attentiveness, and a willingness to listen with the heart.

For many, the reflections begin with an encounter with the messages of peace. In a world often overwhelmed by chaos, the call to peace resonates as both a balm and a challenge. Reflecting on this, one might contemplate a moment of inner turmoil transformed by an unexpected sense of serenity—a small miracle of peace in the midst of life's storms. These reflections can serve as anchor points, gently guiding the soul back to the tranquility offered in Medjugorje's messages. It's not just a call to lay down arms on a global scale but an exhortation to find peace within, to settle the restless heart.

Reflecting on messages of hope, consider the times when hope, like a flickering candle, persisted against the winds of despair. Personal reflections may draw from one's own life or the testimony of others who, inspired by Medjugorje, reclaimed hope amid adversity. Each story of hope serves as a beacon, illuminating the path for others. Here, the reflection becomes not only personal but communal, weaving a connection with all who have walked similar paths of trial and triumph.

Prayer, that ancient and steadfast conduit to the divine, occupies a central place in Medjugorje's reflections. Here, one might journey with Our Lady's encouragement to embrace daily prayer practices. Perhaps recalling a transformative experience of prayer, when whispered words rose like incense, bringing comfort or clarity in times of doubt. Such reflections often reveal the power of the rosary, the gentle rhythm that draws the faithful into a deeper communion with God and a reflection of the divine mysteries that shape our faith journey.

Fasting, too, emerges as a powerful element in personal reflections. The discipline of fasting, ancient yet ever new, invites a deeper reliance on spiritual sustenance over physical. Through reflection, one may recount the challenges and rewards of fasting, the insights gained when worldly distractions are set aside. This reflection can illuminate the profound relationship between sacrifice and spiritual growth, revealing how the hunger for God transcends all other appetites.

To delve into personal reflections on faith is to explore a landscape both rugged and beautiful. The seers' messages encourage a faith strengthened through trial, underscoring the transformation that occurs when faith is lived and not merely professed. Reflect on instances of testing, when faith met doubt, and yet emerged refined and more radiant.

These reflections offer a testament to the enduring nature of faith, a light that perseveres even when shadows loom large.

Conversion, a pivotal theme in Medjugorje's messages, encourages sincere reflection on personal transformation. Reflect upon your own journey, a series of conversions marked by small shifts and grand epiphanies. Conversion is not solely a singular event but an ongoing process of turning ever closer to the heart of God. Each reflection can capture moments of grace when the soul was nudged gently, or perhaps not so gently, toward greater holiness.

Through reflections anchored in the traditions of the Church, we are invited to explore how the messages of Medjugorje echo those traditions deeply. This sacred alignment offers a path both ancient and new, rich with the wisdom of saints and the teachings of the Church. Personal reflections might explore the comfort found in tradition, an embrace that holds yet also propels one towards continual spiritual renewal.

In crafting these reflections, consider the allegories and symbols that arise from one's spiritual journey. The creators of such reflections are akin to artists, painting with words and imbuing each line with divine inspiration. The techniques for writing spiritually-inspired reflections include an openness to the Spirit, an attentiveness to the whispers of the heart, and a skillful weaving of personal experience with universal truth.

Ultimately, these reflections for personal use are invitations—personal invitations to engage more deeply with one's faith journey. They are crafted, not as completed tales, but as beginnings, as frames for the continuous unfolding of God's work in our lives. Each reflection stands as a signpost on the pilgrim path, pointing toward that which is sacred and true.

By stitching together these reflections, the faithful construct a spiritual fabric that not only adorns their inner sanctuaries but also invites others to gaze upon and find inspiration. This work of reflection is a sacred art, a continual conversation with the divine, an ever-deepening response to the messages and visions of Medjugorje.

Chapter 24: Medjugorje in Art and Culture

In the vibrant system of human creativity, Medjugorje has woven a distinctively spiritual thread that captures both the divine mystery and profound cultural resonance of the apparitions. Artists, inspired by the celestial messages and transformative experiences associated with this sacred place, have created works that mirror the ethereal and tangible entwining of heaven and earth. From solemn paintings capturing the radiant presence of Our Lady to evocative sculptures symbolizing the hope and peace rendered by the messages, Medjugorje has become a wellspring for artistic expression that transcends mere visual beauty, striving to reflect the ineffable grace of divine interaction. Cultural interpretations, spanning across literary and musical realms, also emerge as an allegorical dialogue between faith and artistry, pushing the boundaries of how spiritual truths are perceived and internalized. This infusion into art and culture not only testifies to the deep impact of the Medjugorje phenomenon but also acts as a cultural narrative that holds a mirror to humanity's perpetual quest for the sacred, affirming for believers the heavenly origin and ongoing relevance of the apparitions in contemporary society.

Artistic Representations and Interpretations

Medjugorje, with its profound celestial encounters, has inspired a multitude of artistic representations across various mediums, inviting artists to explore spiritual dimensions within their creations. These artistic endeavors strive to convey the depth of the divine mystery that the seers of Medjugorje experienced, encapsulating their visions in forms that transcend written and spoken language.

The essence of Medjugorje has been captured in art forms as varied as painting, sculpture, and music. Each piece reflects an attempt to bridge the earthly and the divine, providing a tangible representation of the ineffable. Artists, akin to modern-day prophets, channel the ethereal into their work, striving to evoke the reverence and peace that characterize the apparitions. In this pursuit, art becomes a silent yet profound form of meditation, inviting the faithful to contemplate the heavens.

Traditional painting captures the ethereal beauty of the Virgin Mary as described by the seers, bathing the canvas with celestial light and serene expressions. These paintings often depict scenes imbued with symbolic elements drawn from Sacred Scripture, weaving a narrative that connects the viewer to the historical continuum of Marian apparitions. The play of light and shadow in these works alludes to the revelation of divine truth piercing through the veil of worldly obscurity.

Sculpture, on the other hand, offers tactile interaction with the sacred. Carved from stone or molded in clay, these works stand as silent sentinels to the devotion spurred by the events in Medjugorje. The solidity of sculpture speaks to the enduring nature of faith, a testament woven in marble or bronze. Each chisel mark is a prayer; each polished surface, a testament to the permanence of the divine.

In the realm of music, compositions flourish with heavenly influence, transforming the recounted messages into harmonious melodies and resonant chorales. Music, in its ethereal nature, elevates the soul, echoing the messages of peace and hope imparted by the Virgin. Choirs and soloists alike harness rhythm and melody to transport listeners to the ethereal moments of divine visitation, reenacting the sublime resonance of celestial voices through earthly art.

The dramatic arts also serve as a channel through which the events of Medjugorje are reimagined and explored. Theatrical performances, infused with allegorical narrative, delve into the mysteries of the apparitions, allowing audiences to engage with the emotional and spiritual facets of the phenomena. Through dialogue and movement, these dramatizations portray the transformative power of divine interaction and the spiritual awakening it fosters in those who witness it.

Literature, though not traditionally visual or auditory, captures the essence of Medjugorje in prose and poetry. Writers imbued with spiritual conviction craft narratives and verses that reflect the mystical experience of the seers. Words become vessels carrying the reader into realms of contemplation and introspection, urging them to reflect on their relationship with the divine and the eternal truths expressed in those miraculous encounters.

Throughout these artistic endeavors, the guidance and inspiration found in Sacred Tradition and Sacred Scripture are evident. Artists often draw upon biblical imagery and Marian symbols, creating works that resonate with the faithful and scholars alike. This sharing of symbols and themes strengthens the perception of Medjugorje's messages as aligned with the broader deposit of the Church's teachings.

While these representations strive to depict the indescribable, they also challenge the observer to delve beyond the surface. To appreciate these artworks is to engage in a dialogue between the physical and metaphysical, the seen and the unseen. In this manner, art serves as both a mirror and a window, reflecting personal faith while opening it to the infinite gaze of divine love.

As Medjugorje continues to be a fountain of spiritual renewal, its portrayal in art will undoubtedly evolve. Future artistic interpretations will likely explore new mediums, incorporating emerging technology and innovative expressions to retell the story of these heavenly encounters. Just as the messages of Medjugorje have traveled across the world, these artistic interpretations continue to expand, inviting each new generation to engage with the mystery anew.

Ultimately, the artistic representations of Medjugorje stand as a testament to the profound impact of divine revelation on the human soul. Through art, the sacred messages delivered in a small Bosnian village transcend linguistic and cultural boundaries, leaving a lasting imprint on the hearts of believers. This transcendent art fosters a contemplative engagement with the mystery of faith, inviting individuals to journey inward into their spiritual lives and outward into the world as messengers of peace and hope, much like the seers themselves.

Cultural Impact of the Messages

The cultural impact of the messages of Medjugorje extends beyond the boundaries of faith, leaving an indelible mark on the collective consciousness. This phenomenon is not confined to religious communities but has permeated various aspects of art, literature, and even popular culture. Indeed, the messages delivered by Our Lady speak not only to individual souls but also to the broader human experience, calling for reflection, renewal, and a deeper understanding of the human condition.

The powerful narratives of the apparitions have inspired numerous works of art, transcending religious imagery to touch universal themes of peace, hope, and redemption. Painters, sculptors, and digital artists alike have drawn on these messages to create visually stunning works that capture the ethereal and transformative nature of these divine encounters. One can find these works adorning chapels, galleries, and even public spaces, serving as sacred reminders of the spiritual renewal that Medjugorje calls for.

Literature, too, has embraced the messages of Medjugorje, with authors weaving them into novels, poetry, and plays. These works often explore the tensions between faith and doubt, tradition and modernity, echoing the allegorical depth of the messages themselves. Through prose and verse, writers have offered new lenses to explore the challenges and aspirations of contemporary spirituality, invoking Medjugorje as a symbol of divine intervention and a catalyst for personal and communal transformation.

In music, the messages have found resonance in compositions that blend traditional hymns with contemporary sounds, creating a harmonious bridge between past and present. Musicians and composers have taken inspiration from the messages, crafting pieces that invite listeners into an experience of contemplation and spiritual awakening. These creations have not only enriched liturgical services but have also found their way into the broader musical landscape, thus extending the influence of Medjugorje's messages beyond ecclesiastical confines.

Film and media have further disseminated the messages of Medjugorje, providing platforms for stories of faith and conversion to reach global audiences. Documentaries and films that depict the experiences of the seers and the lived experiences of pilgrims often emphasize the transformative power of these heavenly messages. Through visual storytelling, they have the unique ability to convey not only the historical and theological significance of Medjugorje but also its enduring relevance for modern audiences seeking meaning and spiritual fulfillment.

Popular culture has not remained untouched either. The archetypal themes from the Medjugorje messages—such as the struggle between good and evil, the quest for inner peace, and the transformative power of love and sacrifice—have found their way into mainstream narratives. These themes resonate deeply because they are essentially the human story, one that speaks to the core of our shared experience, regardless of cultural or religious background.

In communities worldwide, the messages of Medjugorje have spurred social and cultural movements, inspiring acts of charity, peace-building efforts, and communal prayer gatherings. Across diverse cultures, these messages have become a rallying call for unity and reconciliation, prompting initiatives that transcend borders and foster a spirit of global kinship. By promoting values of peace, prayer, and conversion, they encourage individuals and communities to work toward a more compassionate and just world.

Cultural festivals and events dedicated to Marian devotion often include elements from Medjugorje as part of their celebration, highlighting its place within broader Catholic and Christian cultural expressions. These events not only honor the apparitions but also serve as communal expressions of faith, hope, and thanksgiving. The profound experiences shared during pilgrimages to Medjugorje often become central narrative threads in these cultural expressions, weaving together personal stories of faith and the universal call to holiness.

In educational contexts, the messages have inspired academic discourse and study, leading to conferences, seminars, and curricula that explore the theological, spiritual, and cultural dimensions of Medjugorje. These dialogues enrich our understanding of how private revelations interact with public faith traditions and offer fresh insights into the living tradition of the Church. The study of Medjugorje encourages a deeper appreciation of the mystical elements inherent in everyday faith practices.

As with any significant cultural phenomenon, Medjugorje has not been without its critics and skeptics. Such scrutiny, however, further situates the apparitions within the broader dialogue on faith, reason, and the search for truth. This engagement with critical perspectives reflects the dynamic nature of cultural impact, reminding us that the messages of Medjugorje invite continual reflection and discernment. They challenge us to encounter the divine mystery with both openness and intellectual engagement.

The cultural impact of Medjugorje's messages, therefore, invites a rich tapestry of interpretation and expression, affirming the enduring power of divine messages to inspire, transform, and unite. Whether through art, literature, music, media, or communal celebration, the messages speak to a universal longing for divine encounter and spiritual renewal, offering pathways that transcend the mundane and reach toward the transcendent. In this way, Medjugorje becomes a symbol of hope and a testament to the enduring power of faith in a world searching for meaning.

Chapter 25: Final Thoughts on Medjugorje

As we draw to a close on our journey through the divine tapestry of Medjugorje, we find ourselves immersed in a mosaic of grace, where heaven's whispers echo in our earthly realms. Medjugorje stands as a beacon of hope and a call to greater conversion, with its messages intricately woven into the fabric of our Catholic faith, resonating with biblical truths and sacred traditions. This pilgrimage of the spirit invites us to lay aside the mundane and embrace the transformative power of faith, prayer, and fasting. We are called to look beyond the controversies and skeptics, and instead, to focus on the personal and collective conversions these divine messages ignite. Here, amidst the apparitions, peace emerges not just as a distant dream but as a lived reality, urging us to be vessels of change in a restless world. In these final thoughts, let us unite in the shared mission of living out these heavenly communications, finding in them our personal march towards holiness, and nurturing a world thirsting for authentic love and peace. Indeed, Medjugorje is not merely a place; it is a call to action, a vibrant testament to faith alive, urging us to inscribe its lessons onto the tablets of our hearts.

Summarizing Key Messages and Lessons

The arc of divine whispers woven throughout the unfolding narrative of Medjugorje has formed a rich oracle of spiritual enlightenment, intricately bound by threads of peace, prayer, and transformation. From the very onset, the messages bestowed upon the seers have transcended mere words, resonating deeply within the hearts of countless believers who have found solace in these heavenly exhortations. These messages beckon the faithful to embark on a contemplative journey, seeking not only personal growth but also a profound connection with the Sacred Heart of Christ through the Immaculate Heart of Mary.

Among the most salient lessons drawn from the sequence of messages is the call to profound peace. Not a superficial absence of conflict, but a peace that permeates the soul, drawing it towards divine tranquility. This peace aligns seamlessly with Christ's exhortation in the Gospels, where He offers a peace unlike any the world can give. It invites believers to cultivate a serene heart amid the cacophony of modern life, urging them to become vessels of this peace, bringing light to an often tumultuous world.

Prayer emerges as another cornerstone of the Medjugorje messages, echoing the perennial wisdom of the Church Fathers and the profound simplicity found in Saint Therese's "Little Way." The messages emphasize prayer not only as a ritual but as a living dialogue with the divine, a sacred practice that transforms the mundane into the holy. The Rosary, a central prayer practice highlighted by the apparitions, becomes a spiritual lifeline that connects the individual soul to the broader cosmic narrative of Christ's salvific mission.

Fasting, too, finds its place as a meaningful spiritual discipline, reiterated with urgency within the messages. This act of self-denial is not merely an ascetic practice but an invitation to deeper communion with God. It teaches the faithful to transcend the desires of the flesh and attune more fully to the whispers of the Spirit. By embracing fasting as a spiritual exercise, believers are reminded of Christ's own 40 days in the desert and are encouraged to unite their sacrifices with His, participating in His redemptive suffering.

The messages call for an unwavering faith, a steadfast reliance on God's providence even in the face of doubt and despair. In an age marked by skepticism and secularism, the Medjugorje apparitions serve as a beacon of hope, a divine reminder that faith remains as relevant and necessary as ever. Through testimonies of strengthened faith and remarkable conversions, these sacred messages have become catalysts for revitalizing Catholic devotion worldwide.

Moreover, Medjugorje's messages invite believers to a transformative conversion, a theme that is interwoven with biblical exhortations to "repent and believe in the Gospel." Conversion here is depicted as a lifelong journey rather than a singular event, a daily surrender to God's will. Through stories of personal transformation and spiritual awakening, the messages encourage the faithful to leave behind the burdens of sin and embrace the life-giving grace offered by Christ.

Aligning with Sacred Tradition and Scripture, the teachings presented in Medjugorje are not novel doctrines but reaffirmations of eternal truths deeply rooted in the Church's magisterium. They call the faithful back to the foundational pillars of the faith, echoing the wisdom articulated by theologians like Thomas Aquinas, who sought harmony between reason and revelation.

The practical instructions from Our Lady serve as a spiritual guide for modern times, offering timeless wisdom tailored to contemporary challenges. The messages provide actionable steps for spiritual growth, urging believers to integrate daily practices of devotion into their lives. This practical spirituality helps foster a living faith that permeates every aspect of life, transforming Christians into agents of change within their communities.

In sum, the messages of Medjugorje are imbued with a sacredness that speaks to the very heart of Christian calling. They reinforce the virtues of peace, prayer, fasting, faith, and conversion, aligning harmoniously with the Church's teachings. As these messages continue to inspire countless souls, they invite each believer to reflect deeply on their path, encouraging a renewed commitment to live out the Gospel with fervor and authenticity. Ultimately, the lessons from Medjugorje are not just for personal edification but serve as a prophetic call for a communal renewal of the faith, urging the Church to mirror the love, mercy, and peace of Christ in an ever-changing world.

Personal Call to Action

The narratives emerging from Medjugorje are not merely stories to be recounted; they are cries from the depths of the human heart beckoning a response. In the shadows of our mundane lives, the messages of Medjugorje serve as a luminous signpost, compelling us to step beyond passive observation into active companionship with those visions affirmed by heavenly clarity. Here lies an invitation as profound as it is personal, calling each of us to weave the Medjugorje messages into the fabric of our daily existence.

Consider the essence of these revelations—a construct of divine love, underscored by the calls to prayer, peace, and conversion. Each thread in this spiritual fabric urges us to examine our lives with unflinching honesty and unwavering courage. We are called to reflect, not as bystanders but as participants, challenged to rediscover the divine echoes in the daily rhythm of our lives. The visions from Medjugorje, therefore, are not distant celestial phenomena but are instead a blueprint for holiness we can touch and hold.

Engaging with the Medjugorje messages necessarily entails a deliberate commitment to personal transformation. These are not idle words, but rather a dynamic call to action. Can we, in our current walk of faith, truly say we have embraced the call to conversion as passionately and fervently as these messages demand? This chapter endeavors to kindle a desire within each of us, propelling us to live authentically as artisans of God's peace amid a fragmented world.

Meditate on the simple yet profound call for peace. In a world rife with conflict, the Medjugorje messages echo with urgency—a compelling reminder that true peace begins within our hearts before it radiates outwards to the world. As individuals, we must rekindle a peaceful heart, cultivating harmony in our personal relations and communities. Could we not see this invitation as a moral imperative, a pathway that directs us to become uncompromising custodians of peace?

The urgency of Medjugorje is grounded not only in grand gestures but also in the quiet sanctity of daily devotion. How often do we let the noise of the world drown out the gentle whispers of Our Lady? Yet, these revelations urge us to prioritize prayer, to let it become as natural as breathing. Let the rhythmic chant of the Rosary anchor us, each bead a testament to our devotion and our willingness to be vessels of divine grace. We are called to deepen our prayer life, allowing these moments of grace to transform our hearts and minds.

The message of fasting also beckons us to embrace self-discipline as an act of love and sacrifice. In a society where excess often leads to spiritual lethargy, fasting becomes a countercultural act of reclamation. It is a reorientation towards simplicity and reliance on divine providence. This voluntary abstinence serves as a reminder that our true nourishment comes not from what we consume, but from our communion with God.

Moreover, embracing the Medjugorje messages involves active discernment, letting the Holy Spirit guide our journey. It's a call to embody the teachings of Christ, aligning our personal narratives with eternal truth. This alignment with sacred tradition invites us to ponder a deeper question—how are we living out these truths in today's rapidly changing world? This is the personal task at hand: transforming insights into actions and beliefs into lived experiences.

The call to action issued by Medjugorje demands that we live out the vision aligned with Sacred Scripture and Tradition. It's an invitation to participate consciously and fervently in the unfolding drama of salvation, aligning ourselves with the values of the Gospel. In this commitment lies the potential to become co-creators of a narrative where love triumphs, hope endures, and faith blazes like a torch in the night.

In the spirit of Oscar Wilde's lyrical prose, let our response be one of beauty and grace, sculpting lives that reflect the splendor of celestial love. Let Thomas Aquinas' reason enlighten our path, ensuring that our journey is not only heartfelt but also grounded in sound doctrine. And may the gentle warmth of Saint Therese's simplicity guide us to embrace these teachings with childlike trust.

This personal call to action is a transformative endeavor. It is an ongoing dialogue between the self and the divine, an ever-deepening relationship with Our Lady's messages. This call implores us to break from apathy, to be not just hearers but doers of the word, crafting a legacy of faith that will echo through generations.

Embrace this call to action with resolute hearts and minds, becoming living testaments to the truths revealed at Medjugorje. As we move forward, may each step be in harmony with these divine messages, transforming our lives and, through us, the world at large. In the end, it is the synthesis of faith and action, contemplation, and deeds that will testify most profoundly to the heavenly origin of these visions.

Conclusion

The journey through the revelations and experiences of Medjugorje is one that traverses the depths of faith, the vistas of hope, and the steady shores of spiritual understanding. As we stand at the cusp of this discernment, it is fitting to reflect on the broader implications of these heavenly messages and what they mean for us collectively and individually.

Throughout history, the Church has been guided by both public and private revelation. While public revelation is complete in the life and teachings of Jesus, private revelation continues to beckon us toward deeper conversion and holiness. The messages of Medjugorje serve not as amendments to the Gospel but as luminous reminders calling us toward the heart of Christ. In this way, Medjugorje stands within the rich history of Sacred Tradition, illuminating paths for personal transformation and communal renewal.

At the core of these messages is a persistent call to peace, prayer, fasting, faith, and conversion. These elements are not merely spiritual disciplines but pathways to encountering divine love more deeply. They weave an intricate dance of sanctity, guiding those who embrace them toward a more profound unity with God and neighbor. The seers of Medjugorje, through their fidelity and perseverance, become beacons of hope, reminding us of the transformative power accessible through grace.

The messages also resonate with the timelessness of Sacred Scripture. They echo the calls of the prophets, the wisdom of the Psalms, and the transformative love of the Gospels. In Medjugorje, the call to live a Christ-centered life reverberates, encouraging believers to embody the virtues of humility, charity, and compassion. It is through these virtues that we find our place in the continuing unfolding of God's plan.

In practicing the daily instructions from Our Lady, the faithful are invited to cultivate a spirituality that is both contemplative and active. Prayer becomes not just a moment of solitude but a lifestyle of communion with the Divine. Each prayer, each act of love, each moment of self-denial in fasting draws the soul closer to the light of Christ, dispelling the shadows of doubt and despair.

The controversy and criticisms surrounding Medjugorje, while challenging, also offer opportunities for discernment and dialogue. They urge us to consider the role of private revelation in the Church meticulously, ensuring that it harmonizes with the Deposit of Faith while providing fresh contexts for understanding contemporary spirituality's challenges. The Church's careful response, neither quick to sanction nor dismiss, underscores the need for wisdom, patience, and prayerful consideration.

As we look to the future, Medjugorje presents a living testament to the enduring influence of Marian devotion. It is here that many find solace, healing, and a renewed mission to share the Gospel. As the modern Church evaluates its position and response to these apparitions, it also finds in them a catalyst for evangelization, prompting the faithful to encounter the world with new fervor and understanding.

The pilgrimage to Medjugorje is not solely a physical journey but an interior expedition toward holiness. Those who walk these sacred grounds return transformed, imbued with a sense of purpose and clarity. The pilgrimage experience invites each person to a pilgrimage of the heart, where the divine messages spoken in quiet whispers take root, blossoming into profound acts of faith.

Ultimately, the conclusion of this exploration doesn't signify an ending but a beginning—a call to witness and to live the messages of Medjugorje in our daily lives. It is a herald to embrace the gifts offered through these apparitions, to steward them lovingly within the Church, and to allow them to inspire a deeper commitment to faith, charity, and hope.

In doing so, we align ourselves with the enduring message of Medjugorje: to seek peace with a heart purified by prayer, to embrace our humanity with grace, and to welcome the Divine into the sacredness of everyday life. May the wisdom gleaned from these heavenly encounters continue to guide us, drawing us ever nearer to the fulfillment of God's promise in all the fullness of His love.

Appendix A: Resources and Pilgrimage Guide

For those seeking an intimate encounter with the divine stirrings reported in Medjugorje, this guide serves as both a lantern and path. As pilgrims prepare their hearts to walk these sacred grounds, a multifaceted system of resources unfolds to enhance both understanding and devotion. Immerse yourself in chosen texts that delve deeper into the heavenly messages and their harmonious resonance with Catholic tradition and Scripture. These materials, curated for the discerning spirit, aim to illuminate the rich history and spiritual profundity of the apparitions. Guided by faith, embark on a journey where prayer becomes a vessel and fasting, a cleansing river, all crafted to magnify peace in the soul. As you chart your course to Medjugorje, practical tips interlace with stories of those transformed by their pilgrimages, offering wisdom and inspiration. Within this spiritual itinerary lies a gentle invitation to not merely witness miracles but to live them, emboldening both believer and scholar alike to embrace the transcendent whispers of Medjugorje.

Further Reading and Study Materials

The journey into the heart of Medjugorje, with its wondrous messages and deep spiritual insights, is an adventure of the soul as well as the mind. While much has been laid out in the preceding chapters, there remains a wealth of materials that can further illuminate the themes and experiences of this mystical place. Diverse resources, ranging from academic tomes to personal testimonies, offer deeper insight into the apparitions and messages that have profoundly impacted countless lives since the early 1980s.

For those interested in academic exploration, numerous theological studies and dissertations analyze the veracity and implications of the Medjugorje messages. These works often delve into the connections between the messages and established Church doctrine. Scholars tend to scrutinize the apparitions through the lens of Catholic teachings, often drawing parallels to historical Marian apparitions like those at Lourdes and Fatima. This type of study can enrich one's understanding of how Medjugorje fits within the broader deposit of Marian devotion and Church history.

Books by theologians and religious writers are invaluable for readers seeking to relate their own spiritual journeys to the messages of Medjugorje. Works exploring the life and spiritual growth of the seers provide insightful narratives that intertwine personal experiences with divine messages. These narratives emphasize the transformative power of faith and the intimate relationship between the seers and Our Lady. By reading these accounts, one can gain a deeper appreciation for the unwavering faith and humility shown by the visionaries, who have become beacons of hope for pilgrims worldwide.

Autobiographies and biographies of individuals whose lives have been touched by Medjugorje offer poignant personal reflections that resonate on a deeply human level. These stories of conversion, healing, and newfound purpose provide living testimony to the messages' authenticity and power. It's through these personal accounts that the mystical and sometimes abstract messages of Medjugorje become tangible and relatable to everyday believers.

For those interested in firsthand experiences, numerous documentaries and video recordings capture the essence of the pilgrimage experience. These visual materials often blend interviews with seers, clergy, and pilgrims, while providing breathtaking footage of the spiritual activities occurring in Medjugorje. The visceral impact of seeing the sites and hearing testimonies can be deeply moving, offering a sensory connection to the sacred that text alone might not achieve.

On the digital front, various online platforms and forums provide spaces for discussion and exploration of Medjugorje's impact across the globe. Websites dedicated to Marian apparitions often feature comprehensive resources, including articles, message archives, and user-submitted reflections. Engaging with these communities can foster a sense of belonging and shared purpose among those captivated by Medjugorje's call to faith and conversion.

Beyond traditional media, modern apps designed for spiritual growth include functions like daily prayer reminders and scripture reflections inspired by Medjugorje's teachings. These tools help individuals integrate the core messages of prayer, peace, and conversion into their daily routines, allowing them to live more fully in the spirit of Medjugorje.

To gain a comprehensive understanding of Medjugorje's place within Catholicism, readers might consider diving into Church documents and official statements regarding the apparitions. Papal communications and doctrinal reviews provide an authoritative perspective, enhancing one's grasp of the Church's stance and encouraging a critical, yet faithful, exploration of the phenomena.

Participation in seminars and retreats focusing on Marian devotion and Medjugorje is another enriching avenue for learning. Many retreat centers offer programming that combines scholarly lectures with spiritual exercises, providing an immersive environment for deeper contemplation and understanding.

Lastly, for those called to travel, embarking on a pilgrimage to Medjugorje itself is perhaps the most profound way to connect with the material. While this practical step is discussed in detail elsewhere in the guide, the lived experience of being on holy ground often illuminates teachings and messages in ways that no written word can fully capture.

Practical Guide for Visiting Medjugorje

Pilgrimage to Medjugorje is an endeavor that invites both profound spiritual engagement and the embrace of physical travel and sacred experiences. Situated in the heart of Bosnia and Herzegovina, this once-obscure village has become a beacon for millions seeking both divine encounters and deeper religious connections.

To embark on this journey, one must first consider the spiritual preparations that accompany such an endeavor. It's not simply about reaching a destination; it's about preparing the heart and soul to encounter divine mysteries. Pilgrims are encouraged to begin with introspection and prayer, perhaps incorporating fasting as a means to purify intention and focus one's mind and spirit. This internal readiness allows for a more receptive heart, open to the messages of peace, conversion, and hope that embody the essence of Medjugorje.

Travel logistics also play a vital role. Approaching Medjugorje requires careful planning due to its relatively remote location. Most visitors arrive by flying into the closest major airport, in Sarajevo or Split, and then travel by road to the village. Organized pilgrimages often arrange transport directly from the airport, creating a seamless transition from arrival to spiritual immersion. Independent travelers might choose to rent a car or utilize regional bus services, but whatever mode of transport is selected, the trek through the rugged yet captivating Bosnian landscape becomes a journey of anticipation and reflection.

Once in Medjugorje, accommodations cater to varying needs, from simple guesthouses to more structured hotels. Many of these places of lodging are infused with a palpable sense of hospitality, where stories of faith and conversion effortlessly mingle with everyday conversations. Engaging with the local populace offers invaluable insights into the nuanced history and living spirituality of the area.

The village's focal point is St. James Church, the heart of Medjugorje's spiritual activities. Daily Masses, confessions, and Eucharistic adoration are part and parcel of the spiritual system offered here. The rhythm of liturgical celebrations provides a framework for pilgrims to ground their experiences in communal worship, enhancing a sense of unity and shared faith.

Beyond the church, Medjugorje is marked by sites of profound significance. The Apparition Hill (Podbrdo), where the visionaries first encountered Our Lady, welcomes pilgrims for prayer and reflection. The ascent up the rocky path is both a physical and spiritual exercise, each step a meditation on the journey of faith itself. Atop, a statue of the Virgin Mary stands as a silent witness to countless testimonies of divine encounter and personal transformation.

Another cherished site is Cross Mountain (Križevac). Dominated by a towering cross, erected in 1934 to commemorate the 1900th anniversary of Christ's passion, it is a place of pilgrimage that demands both physical endurance and spiritual resilience. The climb is often accompanied by meditations on the Stations of the Cross, merging nature's beauty with the somber yet hopeful reflections of Christ's path to Golgotha.

Encountering Medjugorje is incomplete without engaging with its community and participating in the array of spiritual services, such as prayer groups and talks by the visionaries or longtime residents. These gatherings often echo the core messages of the apparitions — prayer, penance, peace, conversion, and faith. Hearing firsthand accounts and participating in shared reflections deepens the pilgrim's connection to the divine messages received here.

Shopping and leisure activities are not absent from the journey but are instead woven into the spiritual fabric. Souvenirs often include religious artifacts, rosaries, and books that serve as reminders of one's journey. Dining in Medjugorje offers a taste of the rich Yugoslavian culinary tradition, simple yet fulfilling meals that echo the simplicity of life cherished by the locals.

Indeed, the journey to Medjugorje is rich in opportunity to pause, contemplate, and renew. This pilgrimage, while unique for each visitor, shares a universal resonance in its call to spiritual awakening and commitment to a life more attuned to divine grace. Pilgrims leave not just with mementos of their journey, but with hearts and souls ablaze with the messages of hope, peace, and conversion that have transformed this quiet village into a spiritual haven for the world.